Copyright © 2024 by Jasmine Christi.

All rights reserved with the exception of brief passages quoted for media or review.

Some elements and names have been changed. No identification with actual persons (living or deceased), or products is intended or should be inferred.

Illustrations by Jasmine Christi.

First edition, 2024.
Printed in England.

ISBN: 978-1-3999-8246-7

Also by Jasmine Christi:

London to Fenland, 2021.

Suck Summer Sweet, 2019.

Diarist of the Mundane

Jasmine Christi

2024

"I want to tell you something today, something that I have known for a long while, and you know it too; but perhaps you have never said it to yourself. I am going to tell you now what it is that I know about you and me and our fate. You, Harry, have been an artist and a thinker, a man full of joy and faith, always on the track of what is great and eternal, never content with the trivial and petty. But the more life has awakened you and brought you back to yourself, the greater has you need been and the deeper the sufferings and dread and despair that have overtaken you, till you were up to your neck in them. And all that you once knew and loved and revered as beautiful and sacred, all the belief you once had in mankind and our high destiny, has been of no avail and has lost its worth and gone to pieces. Your faith found no more air to breathe. And suffocation is a hard death. Is that true, Harry? Is that your fate?"

Hermann Hesse, Steppenwolf, 1927.

"Things were somehow so good that they were in danger of becoming very bad because what is fully mature is very close to rotting"

Clarice Lispector, The Hour of the Star, 1977.

Fazed

Now, I must write slowly and candidly, for today I had to unstick myself from the bed. Just four days old these sheets, my sexless sheets. Depression makes everything grimy, the house, touching people, food. I have writhed here in these sheets for days, calling myself ungodly names (names I would not dare say aloud to you). Moronic behaviour for now 25, and still a shadow of a woman. I blew a socket, a fuse, earlier whilst making coffee, so I slammed the door as hard as I could. I told myself (just last year) I was beyond slamming doors. Temper of a fuse.

More importantly—the weather is going through its changes. My hormones, my unwellness, seems to follow suit.

Just last week though, I did have a heavenly day. A little Utopia. I sat in traffic and watched men driving alongside me, a few smiled my direction, I daren't smile back. But I like it when they look. I curved round by Spitalfields and watched people drinking outside pubs I have drank outside of too, then we crossed Tower Bridge. Me and Felicity laughed for hours in the car—suggesting men the other should fuck—insulting men that helped me to reverse park.

I return to my apartment, glowing. I look people in the eye. It was a 17 degree day, the hottest this year.

Now the rains have came and I observe from my bedroom window. I have turned my phone off and locked it away in a drawer. The last time I used it, I started to look at the housing market in Norfolk, then Cornwall, then Clapton. You couldn't fucking tell me what I wanted, for I am one of those ungodly names.

Fickle, indecisive, unsure, maybe plain dumb. A simple, sexless heap of being.

I'd rather stick myself to the bed sheets. I was terrible working at the hospital, I am terrible working anywhere for I like to work in silence, but nurse work is dirty, hard, emotionally numbing. But not having a job is getting to me. Some days I can ignore it, when I walk to the grocery store listening to music, I cook slowly in my yellow kitchen, nap in the afternoon. Then I am in Utopia in a one-bedroom flat.

Even the seasons cannot be persistent. A liminal passing of light and shadow. A passing snapshot quickly morphs into the new present, often faster than I can document it. The earthly Manichean rhythm. The radio was talking about the clocks changing. The circadian rhythm depends on environmental cues. I am astounded to think we are still dictated by farmers, the only people who have the power to change the clocks, to make the mornings light again for work in the fields.

The world as we know it is either heads or tails, a coin does not land on its side. We do our dirty work in the dark. When I was younger and less self-aware, I would keep the blinds closed at times like this, for I was afraid of dust or any filth. An invasion of my home against my will. Chores are never-ending for a fried girl. This morning when I was burnt to a crisp, I got over it, I try not to look for the dust in corners. I turn the speaker up loud.

Devolve, dissolve, perk up a bit, repeat.

Where does that leave me? The wait for a table in the restaurant on a Friday night, the two ciders pushing against your bladder, driving and smiling at men, is this

the Utopia? How are you unphased? Unfazed. Jesus.
Fazed and confused.

Sometimes goodness, most often goodness is waking
up early, drinking tea and making porridge. Watching
the cat stretch and hearing the neighbours awake. My
slice of Utopia if I disregard the unwashed sheets. But
then by afternoon I am bored shitless, I almost always
retire back to bed.

My Utopia is liminal, and I must accept this. It is like a
drug habit that builds, you cannot and will not stay
high.

A Utopia is always interrupted by the powers beyond. I
shall not blame Eve or even Lilith for the downfall of
woman. I am so detached from my sexuality, my
femininity, my gender, I forget I have a womb
somewhere under there. Only 60 years since I was
expected to drop my womb and join the workforce
though, I suppose.

After my bath this morning I found something in the
water. I couldn't decipher if it was a blood clot or a
flower. I keep finding things blown in through the
skylights, which I then investigate in the bath. This had
a little corkscrew tail of brown attached to a thin leaf of
scarlet red at the top. All of life begins in this shape. I
recently germinated seeds for the first time and found
the same shape. These little sperm shaped seeds. All my
pathetic worries and door
slamming is founded and born
from this little shape.

Paradise, I sometimes imagine as
a dirty word. As the greed of
perfectionism. Give me ALL and
I'll sieve through the shit and

write to you about it. Too busy sieving. Then the next day you fingerpick the goodness until you bloat and laze, wasting the days. Like when we were addicts, we wasted day after day, sick in bed. Over performing drained us.

I shall make a hot bottle and return to bed, as the cat would do after breakfast.

Frontal cortex

I peaked at 25
My age of reason finally arrived
He always told me to wait
Until my frontal cortex had developed
Not until then could he marry me
But now with my aesthetic synthesis complete
No more cell cycle—reinventing myself
Better skin better body
Hot mind
It peaked baby

Now post-25
Just shedding
Waiting to see how beyond it I am
I was I am hyperreal—until I withered
But yes yes to the allure of withering
Each morning through the afternoon
I melt into myself
Until the sculptor is home
Then my return to all else
Open the windows wide
Hot bath with lots of salt!
Make his dinner.

First day of spring

I had planned to spend the day in the sunshine. It was 22 degrees. I can't remember a March like this. I went to the print shop and bought a coffee to take down to the river. There is no reception down by the river, so I couldn't listen to the radio. Instead, I watched people and half-heartedly read. There are a lot of kids around. These kids really looked and felt like kids to me. This is the first spring I have felt this. I suppose I am a grown woman as and when I feel like it.

I smoked a couple of cigarettes and decided I was happy on this bench alone overlooking the river, and happy to watch others more than be a part of it. Before I realised my own magnetism for emotion, people-watching depressed me. Old, hobbling couples, incapable of simple chores without assistance. Kids in trousers too small. My eye is too active. I cannot detach as fast as I wish. I didn't let it affect me as much as it used to. I blame the hospital. Sick people quietly existed among us and sat in the parks too. I could smell the hospital on them. That stench of sitting in the same bed, alone for weeks on end. I haven't been able to shake that smell of rotting flesh, age, and neglect. Some days at work I would chain smoke during my lunch break just to get rid of the smell that lingered on my hair and uniform. Only then could I face eating and returning back to the wards.

Back to early trains

I awoke stupidly early for the first time in a long time. I hadn't slept that well in the first place. I had chaotic dreams of driving in the Fens, the hospital, and my local coffee shop. I awoke to check the time regularly during the night, as I was excited to get up.

For the first time this year I am hot and sticky, as I sit on the 08:25 train to Kings X. I must get the underground to Oxford Circus and change lines to get to Lancaster Gate. I am meeting Julz, my friend from Paris (although a Londoner, as he grew up in Greenwich). He lets me edit in his studio, we listen to audiobooks, dance, have dinner.

J and I had been getting on fabulously recently, it was like our old times in Paris. During the summer heatwave in 2019 we spent all day in the Palais Royal reading and sitting. He would buy coffee, sometimes pastries, and we would sit for hours. Later on, we would walk back to his apartment on Rue Visconti to drink cold white wine, smoke on the couch, with the windows wide open and the radio playing. We couldn't afford to drink out at bars. He can now. I like to think I can, but I can't really.

At one time I think I could have loved him and him me, but for various reasons I decided against it. I don't think I could have stayed in Paris much longer. I liked my apartment on Rue Bergère and the city for walking. But I'm too isolated to make friends in new places, I like my own surroundings too much, my indoors.

I like him being in London. The other day we listened to a Proust audiobook. We laughed when the language became close to gibberish to my working class ear. I thought—what would my father think of all this? J is a few years older than my father.

I take lunch in Hyde Park, along that slither of parallel benches or the Italian gardens as it has a fountain. We agreed Parisian gardens are better, except for their possessiveness of untouched grass. For in London, sitting on the grass with can of beer is a rite of passage, when the weather hits 18 degrees and up. You sit for hours drinking a beer out of a can, peeing behind trees, laughing with boys and girls, until darkness at 10pm. London Fields or a village park, you'll always find groups in a circle. For us English love a park.

Spring blues

I reheated coffee and sat in the front room at just past noon. The newsreader was in bed reading the news with his coffee. I had said I would make eggs for breakfast, but the sadness had hit. Unable to make fucking breakfast. We both wondered last night if this mood was in the mail, but I managed to push thru it.

Yesterday I could not manage to eat but cycled to Shepherd's Bush to buy groceries for dinner. I ate three slices of melon and an elbow of a baguette.

The weather had cooled back down to 10 degrees, and I was back to wearing a coat. It felt as if spring had cruelly flirted with me and then declined my phone calls for the next few days. I wished the sun was out so I could sit in Holland Park to read. It was the closest to his house. Sometimes we took a bat and played cricket. I preferred to read under a tree.

I decided today was hopeless. I would read on the sofa. The final draft of 'London to Fenland' should return from the editor today. I should be excited, but I don't particularly care. I remember the last time—sat in a pub on Portobello, I thought—is that it? No joyous parties. Another book done.

I will try to make the eggs for breakfast.

Disorder

I overcame the depression and made myself busy. Busy mornings helped. I forced myself out of bed before 8am and cycled down to Lancaster Gate. Cycling early is very liberating. I took a route through Portobello Road and then up behind Queensway. J met me in Hyde Park for a coffee before we started work at the studio. I loved these early morning starts. J had always been good to me. We always left the house early in Paris too. He said he had the best commute in the world when we were in Paris:

Rue Visconti -> Rue de Seine,
Cross the Pont des Arts (pedestrian bridge)
Thru the Louvre -> Rue de Rivoli
Fountain side at the Palais Royal for three hours on a cold day, six hours when warm.

The Palais Royal commute was for thought, reflection and reading. Not the real work, but all the stuff behind it. I can write here, but I prefer to read and people watch. Now back in London at the studio he was painting on canvas most of the day. Spring was warm again, so we took lunch outside. I didn't have money, so ate plain bread and a plum. I wrapped up the day around 6pm and headed home on my bicycle to the newsreader.

He was not home when I arrived at his Notting Hill flat. I noticed an empty bottle on the side, and cigarettes on the counter. He only smoked when drunk. I felt guilt or some such thing, for having been out all day being productive, whilst he did ?

I don't know what to think of him. He is always misbehaving. He is reckless but with a passion for everything, besides himself. One of these men that knows everything, finishes the crossword, speaks latin, plays the piano, Oxbridge, a little naughty. Past 50, but still. I have been home four hours and he is still not here. I retired to bed early. I would leave the house as early as I could, for I did not feel any joy here. I felt I was wasting my time, and for the first time in a long time, I wished I'd have stayed with J. We never argued. We never dated properly but then again, we had spent two years as close friends, often sharing a room for a week straight, and he had never upset me. Paris emotionally was a blur, but J and I were very attached. We saw each other most days. I don't think we said anything about love. Maybe we did. I can't remember these things. Tomorrow at the studio I will try to think of him romantically and see how that goes. I looked at pictures of us just now, pictures of us in those gardens on the left bank where I was at the height of my fancy with him. Tonight, in Notting Hill, the man didn't even say goodnight to me. Yet here I am, in his home, writing about other men. I should probably head back to the Fens soon.

Eradication

Everything had gotten on my last nerve. I sit on the train back to Ely as I write this. All day I have been daydreaming of getting back to writing in peace.

Yesterday his house was a mess and he wanted to walk with his lady friend, despite the rain. She is my age and has sex for money. One night we walked her dog around Hampstead Heath, drank beer, then that night she cried on my shoulder about her sadness. I was ready to go home to polish my shelves and paint, away from this messiness.

The stress of editing my book had rendered me mostly bed-bound with a headache. When I arrive home to Ely I will clean for an hour. I just cannot wait to be on my own, for a few days. Three days of anything. The holy trinity. Just three. I can paint, listen to records, and read all day. Last night I looked at restaurants. I haven't eaten out in five months, due to the pandemic and lack of money. This doesn't bother me so much, for there are plenty of good walks in Ely and not so many good restaurants anyway. My mother having two pubs, I tend to eat and drink there.

On my way to Kings X today, I was reading Dante, reading about the layers of hell, when then a nun sat next to me on the train! I rarely see nuns in London nor Fenland. I love to see a nun, I often wish I could wear the same outfit all year round, do the same routine and call it a day. I didn't speak to the nun, but the train journey went fast, and soon we parted our ways.

My dad is picking me up from Cambridge to drive me home to Ely. I have missed their company. There isn't one thing that I missed, but I suppose Ely is more so my home than anywhere else. It has all the small things

I pathetically miss whilst away. Perhaps it's the control I miss, the control of knowing where everything is. Bloody trinkets.

I may turn my phone off for several days once I arrive home. I want to do me. Books, radio, and paint. I don't want to do anyone else. That is the plan.

I have no reason to return to London apart from this supposed celebratory book meal I am planning, and to give J his birthday presents. I would like to invite him to the dinner, but I must choose one or the other. Perhaps if I stop by his studio then the other young artists will be there, who I could invite.

My dad spoke of cars and showed me garden furniture. I cannot wait to get in the door and fade gently into my own world. At least my father was back to work now, as the world reopened post-pandemic. I would have more time at the house on my own. I could smoke during the day if he was gone, or sleep during the daytime (without shame).

Fenland nor London wants me. We ate fish and chips for dinner. In the evening I set up my easel and painted flowers with acrylic on wood. The radio brought me comfort and I cleaned my small bedroom that is filled with my parents' junk. It is hard to make somewhere your own when it is filled with other people's possessions. Most of my books I still keep in the storage room above my mums pub.

Ely

I am nauseous with flat
I will come out and say it
Some days the sky is too long
If you told me the world was flat
The Fens would believe you
The sky
My only account of the day
From horizon to horizon
Only this year I noticed the seasons
Not because I am occupied
I am disinterested—rather
Now I have resorted to thinking about the weather
The height of the river
I sit and watch father
Big wet eels
I hate their faces
Water snake
Black gold from the black soil
The money maker daddy call it
I'm going to take myself south
Where the land is round
Bounce
Slip and slide on down
I will go dancing
Men will cup my breasts
And I'll let them
I'll go dancing
And tell my Fenland sky all about it.

I read your Dante on the train but it was wank

I always thought I had fistfuls of God
Especially on the quiet days like today
God in the pockets
Of Nana Y's old trousers
God on my palm
Every time I shake a hand
Give a wank
Wash dishes
A little bit of God slips from my palm

Until I find my palms empty on Sunday evenings.

Expensive groceries

The days have been slow and I know I am slipping. I blame it on the book. It is my sole concentration right now. It will either explode or do nothing as I wait, looking up, twiddling my thumbs. I do not even keep a calendar these days for life is so quiet.

My dad's girlfriend bought me some flowers today as a congratulations on the new book. I have not had fresh flowers for a very long time because of money. I have dipped below £100. This book business does very little for me, and I can't bring myself to work, for four months now. Anyway, they are Gyps and Stocks in purple and white. She bought three bunches to make one bouquet. It looks exquisite and I couldn't be happier.

I am craving luxury. I am saddened to not have anyone to take me out for dinner. I want to be spoilt bloody rotten and put on a train home drunk and fat.

Since leaving the hospital, my routine now consists of coffee and porridge with the radio, then I try to leave the house quickly. I walked into town for coffee and groceries. I sit outside to read for at least an hour or two, sit in the park on the walk back from the shops. Today a baguette, chilli jam, Norfolk raw butter, coriander—which I then re-planted in garden, prawns, garlic, two lemons and an orange soda.

The day was warm today in the sunshine, so I made my lunch and ate outside. Boredom was creeping up and I could not face reading or internet. I vow tomorrow to be busier. I exercised in the garden, as it is a very good day for it, which I seldom see here.

I must try very hard to stop my eyes streaming these days. They always seem to be wet with a dull ache. It reminds me that Nana Y always had streaming eyes too. I have never known anyone more like myself. I am wearing her black cardigan today, her rings too as usual. I should like to light a candle this evening, but it doesn't feel right, yet. I have dreams it has all been a misunderstanding and she is huddled away somewhere warm waiting to reappear.

I am fighting the urge to hop the train to London. It is too easy of an escape, and it should not be an escape. I spoke to J a little today as he is still working in London. For his birthday I bought an art deco picture frame with a recent picture of us, plus two art books from Oxfam.

<u>My eyes still ache</u>

I awoke with a pounding headache but listened to the radio nonetheless. Every slight movement of my head, I could feel a wave of heaviness sliding from side to side. If only it would slip out of my ears or mouth. Plop. I turn the radio down.

I felt my head would slide off my shoulders and slowly melt down my blue dress. I didn't know if I wanted to vomit or a cold shower, something just isn't right today. But I slept peacefully and without disturbance, but that had not cured whatever this is. I drank a cup of coffee with porridge in bed. The radio spoke about Ramadan. It reminded me of my work at the hospital. The parents of the children would offer me home-cooked meals when the sun went down. I remember one particularly delicious looking Biryani—but you couldn't eat whilst nursing. The smells of the sluice just made it impossible. I would eat rice and butter for my lunch, fruit, and water. The plainer the better. Sometimes just crackers with butter.

The flowers in my bedroom made me glow, a change from floating day to day without feeling very much at all, nobody would notice my presence if I didn't leave the house. I don't think I will leave the house today. I will clean, for a clean house is better than going on dates. I stripped the bed and continued to sink into my borderline depressive state.

I have no desire to do anything today but sit at my desk. If the cinemas were open then perhaps, I would go to see a film (if I had the money). No use thinking in hypotheticals though? Last night I watched Taxi Driver on TV. I had read the film script last year and should like to reread it. Good one-liners, and maybe I just want to sink into someone else's existence today.

The day did turn brighter. I walked into the town to drink a coffee outside in the sunshine. I read Taxi Driver and people-watched a little. I didn't see anyone I knew today.

I should *of* been a bird

Train station pigeon
Brought more inspiration to thee
Than the hundred people
In my periphery

If a bird alone
Is what makes me write
I worry that ultimately
The bird is more bright

I take the bus into town
Watch and observe
Write my little diaries
Everything neat and preserved

I am drinking too much
Thinking too little of God
I spend the days asleep
With this head full of fog

I clean the house
Then I retire back to bed
Although these days
I do not wish I were dead.

<u>God as a pigeon</u>

I want sky here!
Earth there!

Publishing day

I am leaving London and am now back in Fenland, for good. Luckily, I have few possessions left in Notting Hill. The only thing I'll really miss are my bunny slippers.

I cannot keep running back because of the desperate loneliness. If I was stable, it would have been over months ago, maybe years. Yesterday I asked newsman to cast a final eye over my book, but he was too busy out with that same girl. When he finally got around to it —he was drunk and seeing words twice, making a mess of it. I just had to tell him to put it down.

Today I just published it. I am alone at home, sat in front of the radiator trying to warm up. I feel pathetic and depressed—constantly on the verge of tears. But I fought it, I took lunch at my mum's pub with a celebratory gin. I desperately searched my phone to try to find someone to keep me company tonight. I wanted to wreak havoc, drink, cocaine, dance, men. All of it. But I am in Ely alone. I will change the water in the vase and dust the surfaces. I want to make it to London tomorrow for a moral boost.

Old friends and new men

In the act of getting my shit together, I cleaned the entire house from top to bottom. It smells so wonderfully clean, and I slept well in the clean linen.

Today I am taking a train to a village called Waterbeach to visit my married friends. I cannot wait to see their new house for they have superb taste. We have spectacular outings and they always write back to me. We've had walks in Richmond, a holiday to Warsaw, long drives across the Fens in the 1969 green Rover.

Tomorrow I am going to London to deliver J his birthday presents. Another painter has a studio next door to him, who I spoke with last week. A very sweet, very young painter. We shared a cigarette, and he showed me around his studio— these obscure big black and yellow gaping eternal holes of ink or oil.

In the spirit of starting my new life, I have made a date with a man from Brazil who is an artist—but it appears to be serious business. He makes these huge twisted wooden sculptures. They look insane. I can't imagine how you would make anything like that. He lives in Peckham but offered to meet me in the Italian Gardens for coffee and a stroll. He seems very polite, and I look forward to taking a walk. If we get along, I may take him to the studio to meet the boys—as J has an interest in making sculptures too.

Friday 16th April

Hand-drawn map of central London showing Underground stations along a line from Queensway, Lancaster G., Marble Arch, Bond St., Oxford St., Tottenham C. Rd., to Holborn, with Hyde Park, Hyde P. Corner, Mayfair, Soho, Green Park, Piccadilly C., Leicester Sq., Buckingham Palace, Westminster, Belgravia, and V & A marked.

Friday trains

The book had exceeded my expectations when I awoke. People ordered from New Zealand, Canada, Sweden, France, USA. My mood lifted.

I got up before 07:00 and took coffee in town before hopping the train. I want to celebrate but I don't know how. I have no money and few friends. I hoped when I stopped by the studio maybe the boys would want to get a drink. I think of Champagne and a mini cigar, on a terrace, overlooking the Thames! My remaining £90 must last the month. Plus, I don't know any terraces overlooking the Thames.

I am selling myself as a person just as much as a book. I feel perhaps as the amoeba felt as the transformation to frog begins after dreaming.

My train is moving far too slow for my liking. It is full of young, attractive people on their way to London.

I have not thought much newsman. I know it will be incredibly lonely without him—especially when J heads back to Paris.

I made my way to Lancaster gate where I hung out with at the studio with J and the other painters. We went to Les Filles for coffee and gossiped. At noon, I met the Brazilian sculptor man in the Italian Gardens. We walked very far over the course of two hours. This part of London is very parallel. I never realised it was a straight line into town from here. Let me draw you a map! I should like to do that walk again when I have money and can go into the shops.

The artist was incredibly polite and mild-mannered, a very gentle man. We talked about everything I could think of. I knew I wanted this. I took him back to the studio to meet the boys and they got on. J liked his sculptures a lot. I can't quite imagine just how big these artworks must be, and all the work that goes into them. They are like twisted pieces of wood wrapping around each other from the ground to the ceiling. Really cool.

He said I was pretty and escorted me back to King's X. He asked me to stay for dinner, but I had made plans for dinner with my dad. He said he would very much like to see me again, then invited me to visit his studio in Peckham and dinner next week. What a charming man. I've never met a Brazilian man, only women.

The day was sunny and warmer than usual, I wish I could have stayed in London to have a beer and socialise. This is the first time in a long time that I have been to London for just the day. It did feel foreign spending just six hours and getting the train home, but I did not feel tempted to call newsman. Plus I had promised my dad I would be home for dinner—we were having Indian food tonight.

Does the amoeba dream of the frog?

I find myself stuck
This internal machine
Always moving
Against my will
The cogs turn
My stomach grumbles
Still I churn and grind
Periods of productivity
Periods of bodily abuse
My body awake for four days in a row
Speed is of the essence
Sometimes I worry it will all end
So I do not stop
If you put your head under water
You hear your own clock ticking

My internal life
Sudden awareness

A dot went bang
and now I am trapped inside this girl.

My desk

The day had no plans for me, except for dad suggesting a kebab for dinner. It was the first day in a long time that I had slept in the middle of the day. I felt the loneliness but partly enjoyed it. Of course, out of habit I wanted to flee to London—but I am learning to battle that. Right now, I crave iced tea with vodka. I need to save my pennies as I'd like to go to London next week —just for the day.

My dad's friend dropped off some rhubarb and I told myself I would keep busy by making jam and cordial. I don't think I am depressed, but I can't find much to do and don't feel like leaving the house.

I have wondered if the Brazilian artist is thinking of me today. I think he very much liked me and our conversation. I'll look up Peckham on the internet later. I have been once, to visit Poppy when she lived there. As a teen I would come to London and she was who would show me around. As children, I was only allowed to go to the shops with Poppy, as she was considered far more streetwise than me, as children that grow up in London so often are. I feel my father put the fear of God/strangers/violence into me from this age, as everything was to be taken with extreme caution. Although with Poppy I was gifted peace whilst navigating the streets of both Ely and London.

But today, I did everything in my power to stay put. I cleaned my shelves and waited for the sadness to sweep over me until it finally evaporated. Tomorrow dad and I would go to Cambridge for a walk.

Return to Cambridge

Dad went fishing instead, but I still wanted to go to Cambridge. I texted my old nursing friend from the hospital, and we agreed to meet. No restaurants today, for I am thinking of my train ticket to Peckham.

The artist says he travels a lot for work and will be in Denmark next week, but apart from that "I am always free for you" he told me. He is very sweet. I have never been anywhere like Brazil, not touched South America. I hope we can form at least a friendship and maybe even travel somewhere together. Yesterday he texted me saying:

"It's very lively here in Peckham. The pubs and restaurants are open, it's pumping. Lots of people and music. Next time you've got, come over."

Christi does Peckham

I thought of Paul Paray and Ravel at the casino in Monte-Carlo. Paray asked Ravel if he'd like to gamble. Ravel declined and said, "I wrote Bolero and won, I'll let it go at that."

I am feeling similar. Again, life has flipped. How many times more must the axis spin? The world's axis is controlled by the will of man approaching woman (me), can you convince me otherwise?

It is 09:00 on a Thursday, and I find myself in Peckham. I have been here for two days and am having the most wonderful time. My mood is easy and life is peaceful. He said I may stay forever if I please.

I would very much like to. I do not have much in Ely these days and I find it depressing. He has been in London for just a few months and is renting a very comfortable apartment in the centre of Peckham. It has very large windows that let just the right amount of light in the morning—no feeling of dread in the mornings here. Impossible.

We kissed with tongue for hours. I think we mirror each other very well. I haven't met anyone so gentle in a long time. I like to think of exterior display as gentle too. He is a proper gentleman, and everything seems to add up. He even eats porridge for breakfast like me. He has made me porridge and it is better than mine—grated apple (pink lady), coconut flakes and roasted almonds. Where do these men hide away for years? Why do they suddenly emerge? I suppose they hide in Brazil.

I feel this writing is dull as I lose my interest in questioning anything. Although now, I shall write about my fears. I fear it will drown out and I will find myself lost again. I haven't known him long enough to miss him yet, but he is going away to Denmark at the weekend for work. We will have tomorrow together and then I won't see him for three weeks.

The day is mine and I have no plans outside of writing and perhaps making a map of Peckham. This could be my home someday, who knows. It seems more and more like that each day. All we do is sit around looking at each other and making out. What else is there to do when first in love? He smells like sweet earth.

I cannot remember the exact sensation of falling in love for the first time—except for the amnesia. The world fails to exist and bother you as it once did. As if all the dust has been lifted and the shadows have disappeared. It is just you and a lover now, with Peckham at your disposal. Ha!

Last night was heavenly—I made my homemade sweet potato gnocchi, salad, cheese, and rosé. We listened to The Clash over dinner before retiring to bed. We slept well arm in arm. Life feels so much simpler with him here—to think a week ago I had not met him. He is constantly kissing and stroking me. I can't remember a man being like this before.

I do not know what we will do today. I would like to visit the boys down at the studio in Lancaster Gate. Maybe have a beer in the sunshine in Hyde Park before meeting the new boy back for dinner. I certainly did not expect my life to head this direction but here I am—sat in yet another flat, with yet another man, still writing. It has actually now been three years of this, this lifestyle yet, evolving under the same circumstances. The writing doesn't feel as natural right now, I apologise. I just want to swoon over the boy. Bye for now.

Stay

Had lots of sex and then cleaned his kitchen (unrelated actions).

We ate out at a Kurdish restaurant on Rye Lane—pistachio and lemon dip, spinach with cheese, fries with pomegranate and half a bottle of red wine. We arrived home late and I went to the studio after dinner with him. He covered a wooden structure in some kind of brown paste. The studio had an upper level where I could sit. I sat on a deck chair reading Derek Jarman whilst he worked. I watched him often, because it was interesting, but we both were silent doing our own thing, in harmony. I wanted to see if he felt this love too, this air of difference now realised, the unspoken acknowledgement of our unrolling events resembling lovers.

I have not seen newzman in what feels like a very long time now. I have asked him for coffee, but he declines. I would like to pick up my slippers and hot water bottle that I keep at his house, but he does not reply. I sense I must leave him alone for another month or two. Despite declining to be lovers for over three years, this is the expected reaction.

I am mildly terrified at this point for I fear the sudden feelings that we have rushed this and we should take a step back. He called me 'girlfriend' in the house. I suppose I should go home today, but life will feel very quiet back in Ely. I do not have much to occupy my time except for reading in the garden and cleaning, but perhaps the time away will allow us both to reflect on whether we want to do this.

He is leaving tomorrow and I was hoping he would invite me too—although I know it is too soon, and he would be working—but that's the adrenaline of passionate of unconsidered action. I am a country girl, with my country Brazilian, in London. Life is overwhelming and I have no money, still!

Coffee in Ely

April passed me without so much as a thought. We were not blessed with any April showers and the ground is very dry for this time of year.

My bulbs had sprouted, and I feel the life pumping again. Hyacinths I planted in January, when the country was still locked down. I am preparing for my move to Peckham with the boy. I know it is fast moving but I can't resist. I feel I have no time to waste for I might die in my sleep—I still suffer from those raging palpitations in the early hours of the morning, despite all of this. Of course, some days I still get the sadness, even in his company.

I find myself battling the mid-afternoon nap, and often losing, for I must succumb to the bed when the days are too long.

I speak to him every day without fail. He returns tomorrow from finishing three weeks of sculpture installation. I wonder if his hands will look any different? You can tell he works with wood, just by his hands. We make love every day and stare at each other constantly. Little pixie boy. I can imagine another little man carving him with a hammer and chisel. He looks so deeply, unlike any other romantic attachment I have ever had. I pray he will always look at me in the same way but alas, love always dies a natural death in some way or another. I have gone as far as to tell my parents about him, they were impressed by his work. Before bed sometimes I watch interviews of him on the internet. I knew on our second meeting, I knew so much that I purposely packed my toothbrush in my handbag.

<u>My old newsreader</u>

He teased me for using the wrong tense
Not getting the Latin clues
The unfinished crossword
He couldn't even mop a floor
Make soup
Make love

A day's work
For him now
Is finishing the bottle
Newspapers
So many fucking newspapers
Words I still don't understand at 23
Cri-de-Coeur, Cunt

Redheads on Tinder
Hide in the bathroom
Swipe swipe
Ejaculate in the sink
Come back to bed baby and
Finish my crossword.

Another Peckham day

Now we had spent three days back together, it was the same as before, you bet that, that same bliss. He is leaving later this week, a sculpture in Holland.

I bought basil, lemons, flour, and a newspaper for him. Once home I rolled the pasta with a bottle of wine (no rolling pin here) and cut linguine into shape, whilst we listened to the radio. Hands sticky in dough is a commitment for not just any man.

Lockdown is over and life is opening up again. I would like money to go out, eat dinner at a restaurant, take him away for the weekend. A train to Edinburgh, drive to Dungeness.

He exercised in the morning and I tried to join in. I couldn't do much, my twig arms just couldn't hold me above the ground. So I spent most of it on the floor, embarrassed. When I thought this hell was over, he said that was the first of four sets done. I couldn't face it and escaped to the bathroom for a quiet cry. It reminded me of my years of physical neglect to my body, due a few years in bed? Bad teeth, bad skin, old (although nice) clothes (but with holes) in them, and then this body. It fuelled me into this hole I had to try hard to climb out of. I emerged from the bathroom after ten minutes and retired to bed, utterly distraught at my refusal to accept time. I slept for three hours.

Tolerable and ordinary afternoon

The linen bedsheets
I know I can depend
My only method
To emotionally mend

Close the curtains
Draw the blinds
Away fly my burdens
And asleep falls my mind.

Ask me

We continued in our love haze. He is quite content with me spending the majority of my time sat at the opposite end of his desk, writing and reading.

Last night it was a beautiful dinner, one of my best pastas with sage and lemon. After dinner we watched The Tenant, which was interrupted by the thought of making love on the sofa, all the way to the bed. I want to jump him now. Looking at him now sat at the desk I cannot believe this fragile being penetrates me so deep when the curtains are closed. Even shy people have dirty sex.

Saturday 24th April 2021

Porridge

He hops! out of bed, with that enthusiasm that some people are just born with, or aren't. Porridge with pomegranate, blueberries, and apple. We drank coffee on the couch, and I watched him reading the newspaper. I try to catch his eye and be silly, wink, pout, anything silly. For I can't read over breakfast with him sat beside me.

The depression has been flirting, especially during the early afternoons when the bed calls me louder than anything else. I try to read, write, but I still yearn for a new orientation. Nothing beats eating my porridge with him. The day starts too high.

It is hard to judge—am I getting better? I feel my writing is poorer as a result of my new routine. I don't miss anything, but I feel very quiet. I imagine a result of the pandemic, as I cannot get a train anywhere (I couldn't afford to if I wanted to) anyway, so we don't have to think about that! Thank goodness.

Alone in Fenland for 15 days

Daydreaming about our distance, we have held, before I was born, your life south of the equator. My lovely flat Fenlands. Hop the equator, and 9,000km later (I believe), both north and south Atlantic Ocean crossed. What time did the sun set and rise when you were young? The town translates as Little Gold. Mine is just Southery.

He

I tend to not write of God
I like to write to the other men

The man that said
I will suck all your summer sweet nectar.

I write to God about all else.

Slow days

I filled the days with all that one can—socialising, painting, reading, and sitting around drinking coffee in Ely. My ambition for these weeks was for time to pass as quickly as possible, meaning I often spent the afternoons asleep and the evenings out drinking beer. I clung to my phone awaiting his call each evening, which often lasted close to an hour, despite neither of us having any news.

The absence forced me to reflect upon the true nature of my company alone, again every few years the forced isolation comes. My petty conventions, to be content is not enough. Those lukewarm days, when my heat is away.

I existed alone within Ely, feeling very light and free of burden. I have known him five weeks now. He has claimed to have loved many women although never married, no children. He said our love was forceful and strong, faster than ever before. The speed worries me.

My only issue is that every story somehow morphed itself into something about a past lover. This is where he reminds me of myself—life is only to be noted, spoken, written about, then the love is fulfilled or unfulfilled. Are we both that self-obsessed we need each other to validate our meaning? At least he has the art, I my diaries.

Where has this melancholy sprouted from? Only four weeks ago I was hopelessly in love with this boy, now I dread finishing breakfast and having to begin the day with no purpose. I have a fear of things finishing before I have barely started them. I must push it all away, the fight or flight. If I do not leave first, I will force them to leave with my words of hatred and bouts of depression. It is always the depression that forces them to leave me.

I am not angry or bitter today, I do not wish to accomplish much, I simply wish to keep myself occupied, without bitterness. Following this, I have been turning to religion a lot more during the lonely days. Not specifically any God, just long deep prayers knelt on the floor. More often than not, they are not addressed to anyone. I just like the peace and quiet of being able to think without a purpose. I will perhaps pray a little today before I go out to take coffee somewhere in Peckham. It has rained nearly every day for the last two weeks and I will no doubt be stuck out in the rain when I choose to leave, I shall have to push myself to spend some time outside of the house to give us both some space.

Last night I did not even want to make love. I was too busy worrying about when and how our love would end.

<u>English beaches with foreign men</u>

Take me to the English seaside
Somewhere that no matter how loud
We parade our love
Nobody is our witness.

Flip me over more times than the tide
Does the shoreline.

Paris, Peckham

The day seemed to be brighter. I wrote the nursing diaries and did the dishes before taking an early afternoon walk around Peckham. I walked the opposite direction to my usual walk and ended up somewhere along a main road. The walk was not very picturesque, but not very much of Peckham is. I walked until I reached Queens Road where I stopped for a coffee in a charming bakery, under the railway tracks. It had Parisian style chairs, but upon closer inspection, it was a tad dirty and there was a lot of litter. I bought a coffee and bread for lunch nonetheless. The coffee was particularly good and a little sweet. I read a little Dostoevsky. I returned home to make sandwiches with the bread. We both worked silently side-by-side the rest of the day. Tangerines for dessert.

Lost track

I cried most of the day for lack of purpose, stuck in an apartment in Peckham with nothing to do. I slept, drew, read, and cooked. These are all healthy habits, but what do you do in-between? Why are the days so fucking long? Split the day in two, can we do that?

Bourgeois boredom of the lukewarm life.

No real complaints. The man continues to be charming, the apartment is comfortable, and I have no qualms to deal with in the forthcoming weeks.

For life is dust on the table, death, leaking shower head, out of date vegetables—rotting in the fridge. But also new cloth napkins, iced hibiscus tea, papaya, wet kisses, he, he, he and him! Reading in the sun sat at cafe tables by the side of the road. I am fighting the urge to sleep all day again. I will write and maybe accompany him to the studio. He is making a stool for the bathroom, as we agreed the toilet is too high, we named it the Shitoir.

This evening brightened up, as my lover invited me to Mexico, where he is giving a talk about his art. I agreed I'd follow him anywhere. He laughed at me for listening to the same song as when he left this morning, on repeat over and over, still from last night. I know what I like and sometimes the comfort of someone else knowing the words warms me.

Summer in love

We walked down from Leyton to Clapton, stopping at
The Princess of Wales for beer along the river. Summer
has finally arrived in London, greeting me at 27
degrees. The walk was too hot, and the half pint was
very well received by us both. Ordered fish and chips.

He found a house yesterday in Clapton, that he would
like to buy. I liked the house too, for it was airy with
wooden floors, a Victorian terrace.

Peckham Rye

Whilst Blake found angels
I found a man
Peckham Rye gave me
All that it can

He saw trees
And meadows of green
I saw rotten vegetables
Beggars, yuppies, all in between

South of the river
I never thought I'd be
Let alone seeing
Angels in the trees.

iPhone notes

My hungover bones awoke me at 02:00. I lay in silence for hours. I am not a friend of insomnia for sleep is my favourite place, but I am deserving of the sleepless nights. I curse that I deserve it. My mind dreams of the worst of human conditions. I imagine I am in a hospital bed, and therefore I cannot sleep. Haunted by the hundreds forced to sleep alone in the hospital bed. Simply touched by everything that I cannot change. Stroking all those rotting old people, in lines of beds. The man that asked for beetroot but died before I could find one. The man that cut his own arms off with a chainsaw, feeding him rice pudding and jam on a spoon. For I may as well too be stuck in a hospital bed tonight, for my mind is occupied by thoughts of nothing but.

I drank a wine, two beers and two vodkas in this wretched town this evening (it is undeserving of the title city today). The sight of the other patrons made me uneasy, or more so life outside of London. A sea of whiteness, drunk on cheap booze. Burnt shoulders and half-nakedness on a 20 degree day. I must escape yet again and be away from here. I have long given up makeup, television. I may as well watch strangers in the pub and eavesdrop. But as I said, the majority of people here are the sad workaholics—that get blind drunk on the weekends. Watching them will bring you nothing but misery on top of all of your other anxieties, for you know you will awake at 02:00 with a growling stomach, aching from drinking too much.

Although I slept terribly, I have awoken in a rather good mood, for the highlight of the day is taking my coffee in town and reading and writing. The town is quiet before 10:00 and I have much peace in my doings, nobody disturbs me or asks for anything. There are no visibly or obviously homeless in this town, though of course there always are—but you are never asked for money on the street. Plus little crime, little life in the evenings. The only interruptions are children (which I tend to like). Upon finishing my coffee, the thoughts start to settle—how does one spend a whole fucking day? I walk very slowly home and read until it is time for lunch, wash the dishes, read, take a long afternoon nap and then try to draw or sew until it is time to retire to the bed.

If you cannot even engage in hobbies you enjoy, how can one work for another, for a cause that is rather superfluous? I cannot. The world is small, and life is long. There I said it.

Occupation

Had porridge followed by tea with shrooms, although not a lot happened. I drew in the living room and left the apartment when the sun became too hot through the glass. The entire side of the bedroom and living room have large windows from the floor to the ceiling, although this made the flat very warm this time of year. I headed to the studio which is far cooler and watched him painting. I walk down the High St and under the railway track bridges, where the studio and a few pubs are.

I managed to fill the night with sleep, but one cannot sleep an entire day too. There is simply nothing to do. It is worsened now by the days being warm.

How can man not feel utterly useless and devoid of meaning? Perhaps a child would give me purpose, but I fear I would not be alive long enough to care for it as I would wish to. Bringing a child for my own selfish desires is the end of that conversation. Too many bad habits for that too.

I scrolled job listings this morning and it made the dread worse. Last night I had dreamt of the hospital. Some people are simply allocated a place, even the bohemians are allocated their place (they wish not to admit this), but there is place for all but the depressed, who don't care to paint, socialise or make money.

Lust 4 life

It has been a few months of Peckham living. It has brought balance and I am now leaning towards going back to nursing. I cannot live on the £180 benefit a month.

However, for the first time in my life I have developed a little fat on me. My stomach is very round, but I do not care. The rest of me remains a stick. I run occasionally around Burgess Park and go to the gym, very late at night, but am clearly not doing enough of either. Before all of this I would do 40-50k steps on the wards, and skip meals out of tiredness.

I do not have much desire for the bed, as I now realise, I have spent many a year being selfish. A child. That self-obsessed age must have came late for me.

Do you too feel a coward for not looking the homeless men in the eye?

My cowardliness forces my illness, my despair and the days spent in bed. I try to look people in the eyes these days.

The rain falls this June, and I am comfortable.

Blackfriars

Buildings made by thousands of men
Just because they could
Often I must be reminded
Man needs faith to make good

On Blackfriars bridge I watch
Where many a life has stood
If only this vision engrained on me less
I'd cry far less, I would.

Summer, Peckham

Despair and days spent in bed yet again. I tried to find a job in a hospital, clinic or vaccinations, whatever in London. It depresses me greatly. For I don't know how to do anything else. I spend my days mostly in bed, and my diet has suffered. The simpler the better. My baby cooks me dinner when he gets home from the studio.

I was fine for weeks and found purpose.

Overnight it seemed to have vanished, and the eternal tiredness returned. I am so tired all the time.

A fox is asleep in the flower box. He has slept for half of the afternoon. We awake and look at each other briefly. When he is awake, he looks up at me, when asleep I only see his ears poking out the top of the box. I too am a fox asleep in a flower box on a July afternoon.

Hackney house

We then moved into Amhurst Rd, Hackney, East London, for the end of the summer of 2022. The house is Victorian with the typical large wooden window frames and high ceilings. I can't remember ever having a window so large. It took two hands to heave it open. We spend most of our time at the dining room table, baby reads the paper and does emails, before going to the studio to paint in the afternoons. There is a comfortable armchair in the living room under a lamp, where I read most of the day, until preparing dinner for us.

I have not been leaving the house so much, as coffee shops and parks have lost their appeal. It is a cold summer the last weeks. I have worn a jacket out every day for six weeks.

The house has a wonderful bathroom, again with the large windows. There is a standalone lion foot bathroom in baby blue. Although, the bath is positioned very far from the light, so I cannot read in the evenings so well. Opposite there is a sink large enough for three of me to wash their face over. I took a bath this morning (my 24th birthday) and did my hair at the dining room table whilst baby made us porridge.
I pondered how to spend my birthday. The only things that came to mind were:

1. Tea and read a book at Barbican
2. British Transport Museum
3. A drink and dancing in Hackney

London exploration

I hadn't been walking around the new area too much, as the house itself was too nice. Although today I am taking a bus Stoke Newington-Angel-Kings Cross-Soho, so I have the opportunity to explore with my eyes.

The house itself is a few streets away from Hackney Central and Dalston, which then leads onto De Beauvoir. Suave name, should research it more. The pubs are painted beige, the houses have rose gardens in the middle of the squares. Women wear boiler suits and their hair is freshly bleached. Found a restaurant with a good front patio, serves gimlets and good appetisers. I eat good dinners in Stoke Newington also.

Baby mostly works on sculptures and comes home covered in paint. I have been reading crime novels and taking care of the new house. The boiler is broken so I must boil the kettle ten times for a hot bath. But worth it. After I have finished the dishes and cleaned up the mess of the day, I get into my bath. I open the large Victorian windows and let the breeze cool my arms and face, as I sink into the bath. I read in the bath and watch the boy in the bedroom. This bath could be anywhere in the world, and it wouldn't make a difference. I remember laying in baths of tepid water in Morocco where you could smoke in the rooms. Las Vegas with a bath sunk into the living room floor. It is the same anywhere. You bathe, wash the dishes, read your book and try to find a way to keep busy.

I still have no job and NO money! I have lived on £180 a month for so long at this point, since the hospital. But if I am in East London long-term, I shall have to have a serious look.

I have hit Islington now and am starting to recognise this route into town. I quite like this street, although would never have the patience to walk it. It takes a lot to lure me out of the house these days, as you know.

Squeaky

I am in the Fens and it is depressing me. I almost turned around and went straight back home, but I have things to do, more importantly cash my government cheque, that I use to buy groceries and train tickets. Believe me when I say it is easier to avoid Hackney job centres and continue my life partly in the Fens for this pardon and pleasure.

I was not depressed but not inspired either. I sat in the town at a cafe whilst I read another crime novel. I have not seen anyone under the age of 50 in approximately half an hour. Behind me is sat couples of ladies in their 70's, a man has joined, the laughter roars. Drink their coffee and laugh, knowing they have put in their share of work and can now drink their coffee in peace. They laugh every other sentence about their dogs and grandchildren.

There's an infamous street cleaner here, called Squeaky. You hear him before you see him. My grandmother used to tip him a fiver every now and then. In return he gave her extra bin bags. My dad lends him a tenner every Friday, which he then returns on the Monday? He spends it at the pub, opposite my dad's barber shop.

I have a half hour before I must get the train to another Fenland town. The girls are taking me for a bike ride to the abandoned army barracks.

I am down to my last £50 so will browse the charity shops for a present for my baby's birthday. Art history book or a shirt, I think. He is in France now, then his birthday the day after he arrives home.

Rotting-Hill

The days were more mellow and balanced. We are now living in the house with a blue plaque engraved with the name Wyndham Lewis. Hemingway once described Lewis as "having the eyes of an unsuccessful rapist".

Here in Notting Hill for just two months, baby is buying a flat in East London, so we are staying with a friend of his. It is a five-minute walk to Hyde Park. Winter is creeping in, and I feel it on my walks around the gardens. Sometimes I take a book to the park, but mostly I prefer at home by the window, watching out at the pub and church adjacent. The grocery stores here are far better than Peckham or Hackney, I can find nearly anything I could dream of, yet I eat soup most days. I should like to stay in this house longer, but we are just here for autumn, until the house by the marshes is ready.

Grilled octopus in Brazil

I am suddenly and unexpectedly now in Brazil. It is hard to comprehend the change, but what else can you do? One must go with it. It is not a holiday, for we are here under troubling circumstances. My baby, his mother is unwell. Fortunately, she is now seemingly stable and being very well looked after here. I was very impressed by the hospital here.

I have nothing else to compare Brazil to, for I have never been to South America. There is not the continuity of European cites, it is a mix match of colours and buildings. The most exciting sight is the different plants. I have seen cactuses taller than houses, rows of palm trees and my newfound favourite called Saint George's Sword. It is growing on the balcony here. It reminds me of how far away from home I am, all of these plants I want to take back to London, where I pretend climate as universal for me.

Whilst in Kensington I felt poverty at my side, despite the beautiful house of my friend. I ate very poorly, for lack of funds and could not take coffee out, instead making myself a cup at home to take to Hyde Park on my afternoon walks. The luxurious element of Kensington was eliminated by my personal poverty, not having the funds for a winter jumper. I have however arranged a nursing job, I shall begin when I return.

I have seen many new fruits. For breakfast I ate half a papaya and a cashew fruit. I did not know cashews grew on the end of a little peach like fruit. A sour rotten peach. I do not like the cashew fruit, it reminds me of the smell of sickness and the fridge stinks of it.

Alongside the fruits, I have eaten the tapioca pancake filled with coconut and cheese. You must heat the tapioca alone on a very hot dry pan and it forms a crusty pancake. It is very dry but filling. I have also eaten prawns, cod fish and grilled octopus. The octopus was especially worth writing about. It was served with roast potatoes and romesco sauce.

Tomorrow we are going to a restaurant that specialises in Bahian food, from the northeast of Brazil, I understand it is similar to Cajun food. I imagine rich broths of prawns and rice. I am very excited by this type of food. We are able to eat extremely well here for the current exchange rate works in our favour. A large lunch is the equivalent of £4, a beer £1 and a bottle of wine in a restaurant for £5. I am feeling very indulgent having eaten so well and being able to buy luxuries, all these luxuries. A nail varnish too.

My sweetheart is very tense, as expected, but we are busy and doing what we can. He has a red pick-up truck! He never told me he had a car. Nor had I seen pictures of his apartment here, I had nothing to imagine prior to coming, I barely gave it a thought as it was another existence very far away, that I may not have ever been invited to. Alas I am at home wherever I am with him. In just six months we have lived in four places in London. We are used to sleeping side by side now.

The journey here was chaotic as it took three flights due to delays. However, we got an afternoon in Lisbon. It is a very pretty and charming city. The architecture is reminiscent of romantic Southern European daydreams I have had in the past. The buildings are mostly yellow, and the pavements consist of small tiles that are so shiny they look wet. We took a taxi around and stopped for lunch in a humble bistro where I ate garlic prawns with bread and tomatoes. We drank a carafe of Vinho Verde.

We are driving through São Paulo as I write, drunk on caipirinhas with vodka and passion fruit. I feel exotic drinking this, washed down with moqueca of prawns and squid. I am thousands of miles away from my London home, only one man knows my name here (and he is asleep on my lap).

The girls have their thighs out and exposed to the sun, tanned to colours I have never seen naturally on myself. I feel vanilla in comparison, almost inadequate for I do not spend time in the sun as I have a natural distaste for it. Some animals are dangerous when they have leisure. I must stay busy and think less.

I take a long time in the bathroom, I wash the dishes slower and browse the supermarket at a snails pace, for the days are long and I think obsessively. Plus, men prefer gentle women.

Half a papaya

I ate tapioca for breakfast folded with an egg, freshly squeezed cold orange juice, tea with milk and half a papaya. The waitress calls me a little angel or princessa. Eating too much cheese bread here.

I stupidly only brought two long sleeve shirts with me, which are both drying on the balcony. The day is around 20 degrees as it is spring here, yet the girls wear shorts and show off their tanned legs. I am cold in the corner of a cafe drinking a hot chocolate with an exceptional orange cake, however it was served in a metal tin, with a large fork. Too rustic for me.

I am craving home for I feel completely dependent on someone else here. I get nervous at the cafe to order, or even at the supermarkets. The roads are illogical and despite having a reasonable sense of direction, I can never remember the way to the Padaria.

We are going to see the Capybara later, along the riverside. Aside from this I have no plans during my stay, I shall read and sit on the balcony until our time to head home.

There is a fridge full of beer and wine, yet I feel shy to indulge in anything here. My appetite is not its usual self and I am missing rich food. In London I lived so poorly on soups, yet here I can eat extravagantly. I might ask baby to take me for octopus again tonight, I want to indulge.

Another girl has arrived with long tanned legs. It is no wonder I am white and flabby, my legs having not had enough exercise since I was working at the hospital last year. It is over a year since I have worked. It is very easy to spend a year doing nothing.

I await the flight to Blighty, knowing I will miss the closeness of the people in Brazil. Is the weather to blame? I imagine partially. Warm weather allows for spontaneity, you have fewer excuses to say no in the sun, as it loosens the morals.

Mandioquinha

Today a vegetable risotto with Mandioquinha (a lovely potato that tastes a little like a leek). Ice-cream with meringue, one cup of coffee. Two or three beers, a gin cocktail with lavender syrup, okra & shrimp tempura with aji panca & coriander, goats cheese on fruit crackers with cupuaçu (fruit), squid both grilled and fried, squid ink noodles, cup of lemongrass tea.

Barely a year ago I survived on one meal a day which mostly comprised of a cream cheese bagel. I have only cried perhaps once during our time here.

We are to move house at the weekend upon our return to East London. I am using this time to get into better habits. I will exercise and eat more vegetables. I miss the cold weather and I will take cold walks in London once we return. It will feel as if a continued holiday, when we arrive to our new home.

E5

I have arrived back to England and the winter welcomed me with open arms. Every year I am overjoyed to get my big coat out and feel that cold embrace of winter, the slowed down time. I am yet to buy a winter hat (I left mine behind in Ely).

We moved to the new house a week ago. The house is far more charming than I remembered. It is Victorian across three floors. It is a modest little place (less carpets to clean!) and I have found peace in the kitchen. I decided the best way to keep myself in check, is to ensure from the very beginning of this house, I am at my very best.

I am as poor as I've ever been, but now in my own home. I am able to decorate it as my own, we have agreed. I have been tight with money upon returning from Brazil, I have around £50 to last me three weeks. I am not allowing myself to buy coffee or alcohol until I am working and have my first pay check. On that note, my new nursing job begins imminently, a short cycle from the new house.

I don't think I can blame the new house for this seemingly revitalised self. I met many people in Brazil, I was made ever so welcome, truly spoilt by homemade meals and restaurants too. This week I had two friends over, plus my father! I cannot imagine how I will make the time for all of this once I am working Monday to Friday. I even exchanged phone numbers with a few people in Brazil. My life has never felt so full of people. I feel more at ease whilst on my own these days, I enjoy when he leaves for work, so I can read in silence. I will have eggs with rice for lunch, then take a walk up to his studio across the marshes. I need to repaint a chipped frame. I thought about making something from my stamps, since Christmas is approaching, and I will no doubt be forced to give gifts out of embarrassment of the alternative. Little framed stamps depicting each person's hobbies.

I must go for now as I must read up on liver cirrhosis and blood borne viruses (for my new job)! Speak soon.

Puke box

Good morning to you. It has been another few days of bliss here in the winter streets of London. It is so cold you must keep your hands in your pockets... my kind of weather! I took a bus yesterday all the way to Tottenham Court Road in the evening. London at night from the highs and protections of the top floor of the bus, it doesn't get much better than that.

I met a friend for a glass of wine in Brasserie Zedel. I cannot wait until I have money of my own to visit cafes whenever I like. I should like to take myself out for an expensive lunch with my first pay check. I am starting work tomorrow but shall not have a pay check until mid-January. We spoke about her romantic adventure in Belgium over the wine, I fear I did not have anything useful to add to the conversation, but sometimes it is best to just listen and absorb. My troubles with men are few. As if I am not content, I leave. After this we went to the cinema in Leicester Square. I wish I could have stayed for dinner in Chinatown, but again, money. I can only imagine what delicious sticky, salty foods we could have indulged on. Ducks hanging in the window, bao bun shops at every corner, deliciously sweet and gloopy red sauce.

So instead of a delicious hot meal on a cold night, I took the 73 bus home (via Islington) and had a vodka followed by a few glasses of wine with an old friend who stopped by the house. Baby said it was too late to have friends over, I did so, nonetheless. That is very square of him, but perhaps a female wouldn't have come over at that time. I don't know if my guest was hoping for something. He said I looked very well and squeezed my arm. I made it very clear that I am madly in love already, to the point of which I cannot consider sharing a touch with another man right now. I drank a glass too much and retired to bed around 01:00 after a brief sudden red wine vomit. Baby said it was not the occasion to drink. I can now agree with this.

Now I am sat at my new desk facing away from the window (what a shame but it fits nowhere else). My porridge has been awaiting me for several hours as I slept in until 11:00. I am forcing the spoon into my mouth, without giving it much thought. I hope we can have a filling lunch today as it is Sunday. I don't so much fancy going out as my head is delicate, but I would like a bowl of hot spicy ramen with tofu and spring onions. However, today I won't dare ask, as I am feeling twee and small, I should like to keep myself to myself and not ask much of anyone (myself included).

As sadly predicted, I spent the majority of the day snoozing in bed between rising for cups of tea and to run a hot bath. The nerves are really starting to begin. I will come to pieces if I think about it much more. For a short time, I was imagining the introductions, the crushing embarrassment of it all. At the last hospital I was not worthy of an introduction. Doctors I worked alongside did not know my name after one year of me being there. I pray it won't be like that here, my spirit could not cope with it again. It has taken me a year to recover from the haunting impression of that hospital, and I am still not truly recovered, as it is impossible to forget. My nerves are really rattling now. I am sure to burst into tears at some point tonight. I am going to stop writing so I can wash the dishes to take my mind off it.

I know I am capable of doing the job. The biggest fear is being forgotten or ridiculed for not knowing enough. My memory is not great. I have read pages over and over the last few days, but I still forget details that I know I will. Hence, I always carry a notebook. I am terrified of being told off, although I know I must be too hard on myself. At the interview I cried on the walk home, for being so dumb, fucking dumb bitch. Yet they called me the next day and offered me the job. They said I suited the place. Now, I must remind myself of this constantly.

Baby is working at the other table across the room. I shall entertain myself this evening with writing, reading, and tidying the house. I am feeling withdrawn still, I can't believe I puked red wine into a cardboard box last night—couldn't reach the top floor bathroom in time. I tell myself every night is an occasion whenever I see friends (as it used to be such a rarity). Now I have more friends and social events, so I cannot and should not get so excitable to the point of losing control. It is frankly embarrassing for me to have reached this age and not know my limit. Mother is not here to wipe your brow when you are unwell, and my baby boy is not my mother. I shall not allow it.

Tomorrow on my journey home I shall try to write to you some more. I will purposely take the bus, so I have more time to share words with you. I prefer the bus anyways in London, I can learn the city.

Spring is coming and I don't want it

I realise now I haven't written to you since I began nursing again, it has been four months or so. London has been kind, the Brazilian artist kinder and myself — not so much. I have stopped nursing for the time being. A client fell in love with me, and it made me despise the work. He pinned me against the wall, in the nurse's room, grabbed me and told me he had never felt this way before. Sex is everywhere and you cannot escape it. People just want to be touched so badly, they must tell you, they feel the universe is aligned when passion is strong.

I am being fussy and concentrating on silly things. I finally established myself at a steady nursing role but the tragedy (if you can even call it that?) became too much and I once again I feel unwell. I felt how I was back there again, surrounded by the death, I cannot prevent that getting to me. I think most women in their 20's would feel the same being faced with homeless, drug addicted middle-aged men every day. It sure made me feel pretty small in the world. You cannot help everyone who needs help, besides you want to help and they aren't too fussed either way. It's the nature of the disease. The depression of the people, that is the burden, it drains the life out of yourself to the point of where you are no use to these people anymore.

Yet again, here I am drinking coffee and writing about the days that have passed.

People will always lust over me, I just cannot deal with people I am trying to help, having these feelings for me, imagining having sex with me, imagining what I look like naked, wondering about my life. This occurs in every path of life, a nurse, a barista, whatever. I don't know what else I could do to avoid this. Court trials for men touching me at work. Clients texting me, saying they want me. It is utterly horrid. I just let my feelings get in the way of everything to the point of where I cannot function. Yesterday I was a mess, a pit of depression wrapped in a blanket for 16 hours. Once baby was home, I had a bath and he washed my back, then I slept the night through.

I did feel slightly better this morning, I could not blame that on anything in particular, the day just didn't seem so terrifyingly long. Today my mind is on sex. I cannot escape it. I hope I don't write like a man. I can't avert my eyes from men in the cafe, I watch them until they watch me, then I grow agitated at the simplicity of lust. I suppose I could go to the studio and paint for a few hours later on. One cup of coffee and then I can go elsewhere. I must learn to keep myself amused for a few hours each day, sustainable snippets of happiness, fuelled by my soul alone.

Beer on the Eurostar

A small glimpse of love and serenity, all in-between. Next thing you find yourself on the Eurostar to Paris, crying into your Heineken, considering quitting your job and hopping the next train back. God didn't make me unstable, I chose to be because the thrill is higher than the alternative.

A few days of warm sun and galleries in Paris kept me busy, although I was mostly hungover. Disturbed by this temporary disruption to my home life. I drank cider in jugs outdoors and ate seafood dinners with the gallery and my baby.

I cannot remember if there are apples at home, the sheets unwashed, the coffee pot clean or not. I do not want to return to my life before Paris now, I fear my prior life will leave my yearning for this weekend again and again until suffocating me. I cried on the metro, his little linen shirt walking away from me as I return to London to nurse for those who don't appreciate me. To return to unwashed sheets. I hope my bicycle hasn't been stolen. If these are the extent of my worries, God I am a fuckhead. The bar is only one carriage away, but I fear I am making this train travel harder than it need be.

Methadone for you and you and you
==================================

Spring opened up to me like an unwanted cold. Suddenly the days were warm, wet, and never ending. The work was hard, the men (fewer women) an endless flow. I seldom found an evening to myself and when I do, I can finally catch up on writing. Well, I have a lot to catch up on. As I told you, the days are too long and busy to afford me this small private luxury of diaries.

Tonight I found this luxury, for I have the house to myself. I finished my chores for the day (the charity nursing and the cleaning) before heading to the pub for a quick pint and diary entry. Is this all it takes to allow me time to write? I could knock out a book a month, at the rate of evenings like this. Thank God for having the house to yourself. I haven't even told you about work yet.

Baby is still in Paris building his sculpture. I went yesterday, but Paris was too hot, and my work called. I went into work and was welcomed by the police. A client had stated they would attend with a knife if we cancelled his medication, so that was a fun start to a Monday morning. Should have missed my train. Following on, people arrived requesting medication like it was the end of the world. At the time it feels you can't survive without methadone for a week, but in reality when you've been a heroin addict for years, a week is a short wait in comparison. People are busy blaming others for how their life turned out, so much so they do not allow their lives to unfold in the way they wish. Too hooked on the blame. I have started letting go of the blame and holding myself responsible for not having a good time. I owe myself a good life and I will give myself that at any cost necessary.

I escort myself back to yesterday in Paris. I started the morning at Les Deux Magots 9am sharp. I ordered a coffee with milk, a fruit salad, a small baguette with butter and jam, an orange juice and an omelette with cheese. The omelette arrived with a solitary half baby tomato, nonetheless it was perfect. We sat opposite each other inside and watched the child next to me drinking a hot chocolate. I asked my dear:

"Imagine being a child, having breakfast in a place like this. Did you ever have that?"

We confirmed we both did not have that. I would go to the local chip shop (located approx eight miles from our village) for a plate of chips with vinegar on a Saturday night. Baby said he would go to the local pizza parlour, in Ourinhos.

I shall return to work tomorrow with the drug addicts and alcoholics. I hope I shall be appreciated a little more than today. These things aren't necessary, I start to see them as a luxury, like going on a bender at the weekend and then begging your doctor for a benzo to help you sleep. It's a luxury, your own self-pity begging for some relief from your selfishness. Are we deserving of this? I do not know. This is why I continue to work. I cannot know and cannot judge.

23 degrees today, 27 due tomorrow. Tomorrow is a tube strike so I will bicycle, the blue nurse dress gets sweaty and sticks to my back. I feel a certain sense of embarrassment riding through town in that uniform. I'm sure the people don't look at me any different, but I

fear they would look the same either way. That same prying into my life like I owe myself an explanation. I will continue to ignore an explanation for this and continue as I was, on my bicycle or not.

I shall continue my evening in peace and try not to think too much of the clients. Nobody in Hackney tends to talk to me, which mostly is an advantage.

Paris soap

I have made close friends and companionship with a girl living nearby in Hackney, Felicity. I bought her soap from Paris. I wanted to buy mini macrons in a neat little box, but the store was closed on Sundays. I would have brought her for breakfast at Les Deux Magots if I could have.

Back to being a diarist SERIOUSLY. I have been sober for five days. Hardly remarkable I know, but a start. Sobriety has made me realise how very much there is to be done, all the time. All the dust! I cannot sit down until the floors are hoovered, plants watered, the cat brushed. I cannot stand it. I thought even if I had a cleaner and a maid, I still couldn't do everything I wanted to do.

Porridge this morning with grapes, pistachio, chia, and coconut flakes. Three small coffees and water. No medication.

Wearing black cashmere over a black turtleneck, a little scratchy but good looking. My sweetheart said it looks very nice, he then squeezed my tits and cupped my pussy. My breasts are sore, but my period isn't due. Being sober is making me so much more aware of my body and her shortcomings.

Six children have died of Scarlett fever I heard on the radio, suspected due to lack of socialising due to Covid.

Soho nights

I spent the Saturday and Sunday very much not sober and without sleep. I did have a good time, and I feel the same as before I started. We met at the studio, went to the Chesham Arms, ramen dinner, Ronnie Scott's, then a club on Soho (I insisted on leaving), one house in Fitzrovia, another house in Bermondsey, then the northern line and a bus home, arriving to my bed for 11am.

Haven't touched my porridge yet—red grapes and pistachio today. I doubt much will be touched for a few days now.

Work lunch

I scream behind closed doors
Very occasionally on the street
My own poverty of prior years
The extremity worsens on the street
Although my fridge is full
I cannot always share
I allow others to inject themselves
Into me
I give away my lunch most days
My life so simply, so early,
So tender, so timid,
What is one lunch to me?

Studies

The cat is asleep on the rug, curled up in a tight little ball. I am considering a few things today but cannot decide on the order: walk to Clissold Park, make soup and croutons, rewrite a play, or play Pokémon on my Gameboy. That is all on the agenda for today, and that is the way I like it. I am feeling well today.

Last night Stoke Newington was backed up with traffic for an hour, meaning I missed my class. I started a Creative Writing Degree at Birkbeck in Bloomsbury (in Virginia Wolf's old house). It was the one day I didn't leave ridiculously early, because the cat was unwell. The change in plan made me furious. I ended up doing something I used to do years ago, just walking aimlessly in circles. I used to do in the evenings, in Ely, hoping to see men I liked the look of. I only ever found one on those nightly walks. So/but instead now, I circled Euston station for an hour drinking gin from a can, before I headed home. I should be walking more. I have walked more this week than the rest of the year, I imagine. I will make soup now so I can walk later to the park and library. It is so cold I must wear gloves out the last week. It is the perfect weather. I should start cross stitching again. Maybe tonight. Winter activities!

New year

No cocaine on the scene tonight. Newsman joined us for champagne, I did a cheese board. I got fucked last night, had to spend the early evening in a hot bath for an hour to burn the rot out of me, a miso soup, and a litre of cold sparkling water with lemon and a lot of ice, an apple, maybe ice-cream. No cigarettes today. NY evening I turned in early. I overheard them speaking at the front door.

"I am so happy for you both. I know she is difficult, but she needs to be nourished and you've done that. You know she's immensely talented, she just needs you"

I agreed to with his drunken slurry of words and rolled over, to continue to sleep.

Nasty

Rather a nasty mood recently. Not enjoying what I'm reading currently and reading a lot of it. For school. Chaucer. Still sober. Must endure this, do not want to be a waitress or in a hospital.

When I was a child, I was extremely fussy with food, but not so much now thank goodness. I grew out of it, but the fussiness follows you to a certain extent, when all of your senses are beyond your control. Today I refused to touch a chunky salsa—you see like, I'm nasty, I just refuse, self-righteousness, do not bend myself, fussy girls, cannot accept anything other than my own reality. A nasty, fussy, anti-labour girl. Prissy too.

I am forced into distraction constantly. I even considered going bowling today, just to keep busy. I ate a late breakfast then retired to bed for four hours. I ignore that I can leave, I forget I can walk anywhere in London, take a bus or the overground, walk by water, café or grocery stores. There is nowhere I wish to be today.

It's like doing a jigsaw puzzle for the sake of looking at the colours on each piece, for who cares about the greater picture? We already know.

Stuck in Bloomsbury trying to plot time of my life into narrative collectives. I have been so wrapped up in the self. A good time—before you get there you know you aren't having a good time. You become absorbed in one solution, or two if you're unlucky. I push so far, hard, I forget about the weather. Only this year I notice the seasons, and barely. Moods and people alike. Sometimes on sometimes off. For me no excuse. I must always be on. A shame in leaving early. What doesn't she have to prove. My favourite memories are organising my books at home in the winter, early nights with the radio. I push and push to appease. Is this the end of addiction? Allowing the seasons?

Bovary

I have a geranium on my table. No, it is a hyacinth. The brown bulb protrudes from the top of the pot, the ugly, dirty, alien bulb emerging from the soil. As the baby head emerging from the birth canal. But my hyacinth has seven slim green leaves and then the little curved buds of my white hyacinth, that will emerge sometime this spring. They tend to spring early, maybe February even.

I bought it for a few reasons. I had one when we first moved into this house, this time last year. It was purple and I spent a lot of time looking at it. In my worst of times, I also had many hyacinths. When I was forced back into living with dad, I bought six bulbs from the market that I planted in the winter. By the time they bloomed, I was far gone, in Peckham by then. It was the first outdoor activity I did in a long time besides walking. I do not like soil or dirt. Planting something took a lot of effort and mental force from a sensory perspective.

Over breakfast I watched my hyacinth from the couch and thought how much happiness it will bring me in the coming months. I purposely did not buy flowers this week, so my hyacinth can be the star of the show.

I have been reading Madame Bovary and generally being very well the last two days. The house is in order, I am on top of my studies, and I am eating very well but simply. I crave sweet chutneys and lots of garlic but no bread. Rich chutneys to fry eggs, my favourite is coriander and garlic. Too much kale in the fridge, going to make kale pesto for dinner to have with broccoli.

The boy is still here at home with me, yet to leave for work. He is gentle and inwards today, as he is most days.

Schoolgirl at the dinner party

Must start waking up earlier, for I get far more done. Utterly useless in the afternoons. If the opportunity arises, I will drink and smoke at noon which then renders me pointless for four hours. Did a lot of work today though, then baked a cake for a dinner party tonight. Lemon polenta, with pistachio, rose, blood orange (tis the season!) syrup on top.

I walked to the shop before it got dark, again I needed my garlic and coriander chutney, Emmental, apples, bagels and a cider. On the walk I am giddy like a schoolgirl, as the shop is very small, tight, intimate. Two cute guys work there. I get a little embarrassed. I felt self-conscious that I went in the day before for crisps, cider and a hyacinth.

I took the train to Liverpool St where I then walked to Moorgate, not the best walk but fine. I then headed to Clapham.

Chilled Chablis, tomatoes, bread, confit garlic. Then a Pouilly-Fume with Tartiflette. Huge wheels of Reblochon cheese. Very good. It had lardons that we scraped to the side. Leafy greens with walnuts. For dessert my polenta went down a treat. The company sweet, quiet, reserved, kind.

Nurse breakfast

I awoke far earlier than usual, with a bloated and sore womb. My sweet slept until late whilst I ran a bath. I emptied the salt jar and lay for almost an hour. I watched a feather of blood trickle out from in between my legs, growing into a cloud of red and yellow and then somehow being absorbed by all the water and salt, into nothing at all.

I thought of having bread and cheese for breakfast, as I used to, when I worked at the hospital. I looked down at my round stomach and thought another time for bread.

You know—I would sit in my box room each morning at 05:45, nibbling the bread and cheese, trying to stretch time, before I had to walk into the hospital. The lights were not on when you arrived, you crept down the corridor to not wake the patients. The nurses did not speak as we sat together, waiting to find out the order of the day. I would arrive at 06:35, work from 07:00, coffee break at 10:30, then I delayed my lunch for as long as I could, until 16:00 or 17:00. We then clocked off at 20:30. When I arrived home the priority was a hot shower and a good scrub of my hands. I seldom ate in the evenings. In the morning, that little piece of bread and cheese was my highlight of the day, and I think of it now, fondly.

Weather is fine and almost mild. The sky was clear through the skylight in my bathroom.

<u>A stale confession</u>

I sit with my cheap watercolour dusk
A stick of air holding me up
Completely hollow
My legs kick out
A little dance with
Piano keys
Then my toes too
A little elaborate dance they do
I have time to write it down very quickly
Then I hear my heels scrape floor
Blue lights
A skip
Back to where the weather suits my clothes.

Day-to-day

Cocktail nuts
Green juice
Dates
Oats
Green juice with squeeze of lemon
Four kinds of sprout
Two kinds of leaf
Mustard
Cups of tea
Terrible air and worse water here
But the girls are far prettier
The sky must wear a cloak here.

Lapping the life from me
Date to date
I shapeshift
I tease
I return home
I feel I fear
I will be the last one awake
I watch her wet her ears
Feet on the radiator
Watching from the window
I must spend two hours a day at this window
It is facing all trees, no street
Penny sat on my grandmothers dining room chairs
The wooden ones with lime and pink seats
The ones we inherited.

<u>Friday menu</u>

Porridge with pink lady apple, green juice, raisins, dried coconut.

Two fried eggs, rocket, chilli, a lot of pepper.

Vanilla yoghurt in clay bowl. Very earthy vanilla. Will buy again. Belgian the label says.

1, 2, 3, 4 half ciders. One glass of white.

Paella with squid ink, prawns, squid, lemon, garlic cream with french fries.

Leftover fries

Been feeling crooked on earth—three days now. I told myself I will go to the store today, as I want tapioca for my lunch, with shaved coconut and Emmental, chillies, smoked garlic. I will wrap the garlic and leave it in the oven for two hours now. In other times I would ask for a papaya too, but this is not the time or place. I still have faith but must make fewer demands foodwise. Must eat according to place.

Cat is on the radiator, yawning.

Stopped looking at people on the street, it's cold coffee. Backbones do not grow. Forgetting my buzz. I like reading, writing, sewing, cooking, cleaning, and small glasses of cider. I do not like the outdoors for extended periods of leave, prefer flowers to houseplants or loudness (music, voice, or machine).

My cat is always on the radiator, often with me beside. Her cemented routine. Nothing of mine is fully formed like the routine of house cats. I made a cup of tea and saw the leftover fries in the fridge. I couldn't have them with a cup of tea. My baby is home today, sat with his feet up. I hope today I shall leave the house.

Coronation weekend

Coerced out of the house, by the offer of a scoop of ice-cream, grocery shopping and a walk in Abney Park. We looked at the house we nearly bought that overlooks the cemetery. Baby said we should have, but I remember the carpets there and kitchen too small. I have made a mess of my kitchen, I painted everything mustard yellow, the walls, the cabinets. But I still haven't finished sanding the counters or painting one wall. Also would like a rail or two. And I bought an iron shelf, I need to install after painting.

Dinner in the yellow kitchen tonight: roast carrots and new potatoes in mustard, green beans and broccoli in smoked garlic. Nut roast with sage. Homemade veg broth for gravy plus red wine. Tiramisu for dessert.

Did some sewing, reading, took a bath. Thinking about self-presentation when alone. Alone I am not burnt out. My baby wants to see Morandi in Islington. Penny is out playing. Thought about messaging a friend but enjoying my own company recently. Not a burn out. An earned break. Always was like this.

Thinking of taking time in Brazil. A few months of peace, the balcony. The Padaria with tapioca for breakfast. He said his dad would scream if he knew we ate there every morning. Pointless indulgence. I don't eat breakfast out in London, ever. Baby is somewhere here, reading.

I need summer dresses with colour, for my trips. Heeled sandals. A good haircut. I should workout today, abs at least, for this summer I am thinking of. I will buy those little purple fruits with the lychee-like segments inside. Guava juice with lots of ice and a threat of vodka. Corn nuts on the balcony with a cigarette. More Guava juice, then dinner out.

I am happy to be miserable in the occasional different place. São Paulo or Clapton is fine. I now need an itty-bitty bit of sunshine and isolation. I would like to stay here for the Coronation. Sandwiches and a cream sponge. Jam. Sparkling wine. Crisps. With my dear friend Freya who is coming to visit.

Chaos, Earth, Love

Bought a bagel on the walk—with dates, butternut squash and mozzarella, some kind of pesto. A coffee too. Then took a bus to the Estorik collection. Bought a Morandi postcard, had to. Love buying postcards to use as bookmarks or wall art and such. Walked into Islington afterwards, particularly enjoyable walk. I always forget the canal walk near Canonbury. Once in Angel I bought a book on medieval embroidery, a John Fowles and two Plato. Started with Plato in the evening in bed, then again on the floor this morning, against the radiator.

Need to take a bus into Euston, spend the day at the library ASIDE from the diaries. I am absorbing a lot right now. Constant stimulation alone without people. I have turned down all dates, I have piles of thoughts everywhere on the desk. Underlining the good ones with a yellow pencil. Then I'll visit the art shop on Brewer St for oil pastels, to sketch the medieval embroidery onto paper. Need to do something with my hands once a month. Although I find most arts too messy. No plans for lunch, considering a Korean hot dog with cheese. Or a salad at the cafe with the lights in Bloomsbury. Or dumplings, with roti. Focus on my own words. Absorbing and spitting out as I feel best. Haven't bought cigarettes for four days. Listening to music louder than usual.

Anywho, last night I was watching a Brazilian film from the 70's. Baby was pissed I didn't tell him, so he could have joined. I just watched it in the kitchen whilst I was cooking. More nut roast and green beans for tea. I cannot imagine him in Brazil in the 70's. I cannot imagine the scenery alone much different to how I see his home now. He has been looking at me more, especially from the side. He will stare for three or four seconds before looking away. He will kiss my hand whilst I am occupied. We shared one cup of coffee yesterday, he was looking at me from the side then. In the evening we had Brittany cider and red wine before bed.

I clean the floors each day, then the rest is for myself to focus and reflect. I potter up and down the stairs trying to document in the right order. I sit down and think of three words I need to remember the next day. Like Hesiod telling me Chaos, Earth, Love is the correct order. I am EARTH in this list of deciding factors. Then someone said there is no greater benefit than finding a worthy lover from early youth. Tick. Pure obsessional. Over that. Then I practise a speech of dedication for my lover. Thoughts of friends, my face, I force you into the thoughts. Write fast.

Gotta go, bus to catch.

<u>Mapping the thoughts of a woman
obsessed with control that cannot accept
Gods' intervention</u>

What should have been
Habitual
Automatic

As opposed to
Accidentally
Faulty

Allowing pleasure
Prolonged anticipated
Absolute certainty
Predicted, prevented
Social notes
Recipes
Diaries
Bring me peace.

Push for the pub

We went into Soho bowling. Afterwards ate BBQ for dinner. I ate fried cornbread, on the recommendation of my mother—who grew up in the USA. In the bathroom I asked her to order the chicken wings to share, so I could sneak one or two. On these very rare occasions I crave meat and occasionally submit. I drank wine, beer, a gin cocktail, champagne, then a vodka lemonade slush puppy. It didn't touch the sides. We ended up in Finsbury Park homebound. I cannot stand it. Wet dark poverty, one of my least favourite stations in London. I took a bus homebound to Clapton from there. I had to depart the bus early, purely to scream in the street, the wetness of the night had ruined me. I ran across the street as fast as I could without looking.

Before we went out, I put on my grandmother's perfume. I wondered if it would upset mother more than please her, but I doubt she noticed as she didn't say, but she is quiet.

Since this night, I am back to being fearful and avoiding the town. Today I pushed myself to walk to the pub. I watched TV for an hour until I built up the courage or effort. Nobody looked at me and I sat in the corner for two hours drinking cider and reading Lispector. My baby is in Nantes, building a sculpture, the house is silent.

Wild Garlic season

He is painting and talking to me about youth and my complexes, then he said I am older and should know better than to waste my time.

It was so bad today, I taped my face. I spent an hour in the bathroom plucking, rubbing, stretching. I hitched my face back and stuck it in place with medical tape. I cooked breakfast with my face taped. I can still feel it. Two blood vessels burst on my right cheek. Must stop this nonsense out of boredom.

"Don't touch my computer! Or it will be full of pussycats..." he whispers across the room.

I fried the wild garlic with eggs, sesame oil and chilli honey. The shops nearby do not do good bread. I have been craving Turkish bread or challah with blueberry jam. The daytimes feel detached but are speeding by. I am doing the bare minimum with lots of baths. I cried in bed for three hours, then a small interval followed by another two. I screamed under the pillow at my lack of appreciation for nature, writing, knowledge, reading the newspaper, daily habits, exercise, men, and friends.

Daughter

One night, quite far in, he told me his mother had wanted him to date an English girl. Him being a chef, he had wanted to meet the daughter of a restauranteur. He was a chef, as I said, for my mum, but my mother hired him and took him under her wing in this new country. She asked me to take him to Cambridge to show him around. Then he asked me to take him to London, so I did. The usual places, Covent Garden, Camden market—before I go where I go now. He asked if I'd like to see a movie after. I would, but I wouldn't be allowed out past 10. He called my mother, and she said it was fine. We fucked me in the cinema and left with blood all down his jeans. A week later he asked if I would meet his mother. I would, but I'm not allowed. He called my mother and she said it was fine. We took a train across the country there, from Warsaw. We didn't go to the cinema but we did fuck in the train toilet. I have no desire to hide the details from you. Laugh with me. I stayed in Poland for a month on another occasion. I did not have much going on in Ely. But now I have done far greater. I moved to Paris for a man. I went further and farther. South America for a man. Since then I washed up in East London. My dad said I only like exotic men. Small town girl. What do you expect?

Inconvenient woman

I opened my laptop before 07:30 and made excuses to myself as to why I cannot write here. Imagine slogging it to the desk, in the middle of the night, to write with pencil. A blunt, schoolgirl, grubby old pencil. The diary is chaotic. I cannot remember the orders of things.

Going to hot yoga today, it makes you sweat so good. A baptism in their hot haven, cocooned under a train bridge in Hackney. Baking oatmeal cookies. Making wild garlic pesto. Just errands today. Changed to cream candles, bored of the black, far prefer it. I wasn't meant to be writing about this now. What I wanted to be writing about—methods of writing. I need to churn it my diaries through a detached object, a unifier. It makes them into anybody's words, and then I can crack on, having gagged them up, rid of the thought. Leaving something in pencil is barely detaching it from myself at all. It looks at me from a pile telling me to revisit it, I just want to write pages new. The branches out the window are lighter and varying in shade, when before they were a unified library green.

It is later in the morning now. I am going to have to lock myself in a room, just to churn this diary out. I cannot stand revisiting. I need to cut 20 or 30 pages of horribleness, all that before I lived here. I want to vomit. Do musicians listen to their own music? My thoughts are very much alive and deserve the documentation. Just staring at this white screen of orderly lined alphabet, my familiar words, I feel a little at ease, and forget about the dust in the corner of the skirting boards. I am for sure getting more unwell. I may need to move. I may need to go sober. I don't want to upset Penny. She is asleep on the sofa.

I went to hot yoga, sweated out the outside world. I am as red as a plum. I bought groceries and a tin of sardines for Penny. I have taken a seat in the cemetery behind St Augustine tower. My favourite cafe around here. It is a spring day, and the grass has taken that teal colour like it does in the fens. There are daffodils around the trees. I bought some for the house too.

Turns out Penny and daffodils don't agree. I left them in a vase for the downstairs neighbours. Following this, I have been thinking, in my steamy hot bath. I then went to the gallery but quickly returned home, but more about that soon. First, for you, my idealisation tower, my uphill struggle. As a child, I boasted at school that I had gone to London on Sunday—even my dad cancelled the trip last minute.

Now I float or slump (no in between here, madam) around Clapton, drinking, cooking, shopping, exercising. Then I lay in bed and tell you off for the unsolicited advice. I am doing as I wished the year before etc. If I wanted to be a convenience checkout lady I could, and you can't say shit, because it is my world, my ideals. Relaxation. A life of relaxation. Cinema once a month. Pub once a month. Fancy soap. A new summer dress each season. Beep beep as I scan your truffle crisps and 05:00 six pack of lager. Beep beep inconvenient woman in a convenience store. Speak tomorrow.

ECG

To simplify the mechanics of the story arc:
We rise to good fortune
Caused or received
We sink when this fortune changes
For liminal movements make us awake
The wave up and down
Differing speeds and extremity

As a young nurse I gave ECG's
I watch the seemingly normal
Peaks and waves
Unique to each person
Can't read your vinyl lines
Doctors job hun
I'm wearing a fucking baby blue dress
Cinched at the waist

On the night shifts
I would purposely walk very slowly
Down the many corridors
And pretend to look out the window
Anything to be away from that ward.

Trip

Now, my version of a fine time. It's been subconsciously in my mind for months, that girl, she shucks oysters in Whitstable. She too has her own graph of emotional highs, lustful thoughts, and disappointing affairs. I am thinking to myself how much I'd like to visit Whitstable, so I buy a train ticket.

But first I stop at Seaford. I walk over the Seven Sisters Cliffs. Beautiful sea views and a good temp, around 16c with light wind. I walk with headphones anyway. I walk 18km until reaching the town of Eastbourne. I order haddock and chips, with lager. I stay in a seaside Victorian hotel. Very pleasant.

The next day took a train to Hastings, which is by the sea also. Saw the ruins, went to the town of Battle, visited the old monastery. Very remarkable building to be inside of. Museum there too etc. Hotels options in Hastings unremarkable.

Carried onto Canterbury, gorgeous architecture and very consistent. Cathedral worth a visit alone. Hotel very acceptable, 17th century and cosy. Long walks and pub evening in Canterbury today.

Took a remarkably speedy 30-minute bus to Whitstable where I spend the day slurping oysters in a barn with red and white tablecloths. I walk to Herne Bay and back. It is my utopia for one day. That English coastal blue and orange. It could be the desert with Jack Nicholson colours too. I drank a pint of cider at the first pub I found 'The Neptune', which is facing the sea. I smoked a cigarette and planned where to eat next. I stayed at the first hotel I found. The left side of the bed faced the sea and a public walkway. I purposely undressed with the curtains open that next morning. Very slowly. I looked a dogwalker in the eye.

Now, if I repeat this day, I will find myself staring at the ceilings at 5pm edging towards screaming or thumping walls. But consistency moulds identity. I have many ideas, passions, it feels my identity has oozed out every crack to something unrecognisable. Impossible to be categorised as one type of apple— nurse or writer or religious maniac or housewife or drug addict. Today my apple is oyster shuckerrrrr. The cracks in my hands stiffen and itch from sea water. I reach into the ice bucket to shuck the next. I cut the shallots for the mignonette. Father shouts at me to work faster. We sit down at the table and slurp up the leftovers. My bedroom is cold with sea wind. I have never set foot in a hospital. Heaven only lasts a day baby. Onto the next.

Seven Sisters, England, 2023.

Hackney summer

I donated my last days of summer in London to the house and my seemingly growing domesticity. It had not been planted, but any who, it grew over the last two years—in my small haven of Clapton. I fear it was planted as a child by my erratic grandmother, the cleaning one.

Transcendence of the senses had failed me today and I had to resort to depending on myself for amusement. The usual bandits were eradicated. The house feels empty and bare, as I shall return not until September. I ran a bath that is far too hot for June, I crouched in it for fifteen minutes talking to myself, I practically levitate in it for the light here is so light. Levitate up two flights of stairs and into the bath, every six hours. But Brazil has its own light and bathrooms, less stairs. I looked at photos of me in Brazil the last time, I add new words to my pocket notebook:

Eu limpo como minha avó.

I walk to the graveyard cafe, I sit for 40 minutes reading Lispector.

Got a job for two months (for Brazil money). 8pm-8am in a care home in Bow, as grim as it sounds. Someone keeps prank calling me on the night phone that I have to carry all night. The same man, asking if I'm married. They asked me to be night manager on my second shift, so I said fine, just for two months.

Tea, biscuit, snooze.

Edith had sunk so deep into the chair, I imagined her spine mirroring the brown suede curvature, glued as one, a conjoined slump of parallel age. Her shrunken little white head fell into her bony chest. I squinted to watch her closely, your heart sinks, but thank fuck, I saw a breath. A union jack pin on her cardigan leftover from the King's Coronation last week. I smiled— maybe with a little guilt? She was one of the few here that could and would talk, although our conversation was limited to domino game talk and requests for rich teas. She was stern but fair, as she did not care to be called darling.

You see, just like that, I sit here, and these trails come, I follow them, I forget about the life of the people in front of me, I follow them in my head, I write about them quickly. I forget how delicate, how needy they are, here now. I forget that they are not here as I am. Will I ever see where they are?

I watch them snooze. I practice conversations in Portuguese, I think of my summer in Brazil and the people I will meet, I think of my Brazilian waiting for me. I think of the things I'll do to prevent myself ever living here. I'll exercise vigorously, no processed foods, no meat, no sugar in tea. I'll read before bed every night, sudoku, all that shit. I'll stay with my boyfriend. He always tells people he dates a nurse, so that he has someone to look after him. He always says that when they ask if I'm an artist too. Edith tells me I am late, for it is time for the tea trolley. They need not know I am never really here either. I'm gently floating elsewhere too.

Heatwave

I lay in a puddle of my own misery for the remainder of July. I lay on soft linen sheets I could never afford.

I try to read, for two men have told me if I refuse to do anything else, I should at least be reading. For a month now I have promised myself I will run errands in the town. I have not eaten a hot meal for a while now. I float float through summer as I always do. Please bring me back short days of romantic affairs.

My life in London is a pathetic vision of misery. But the girls here are far prettier. The air not as pure as I'm used to. Lapping the life from me each dumb date at a time. Drinks, cigarettes, cocaine and home time. I can always stay up the latest when everybody has had their fun and returns to reality. I feel I will be the last one awake for the rest of my days. Lapping up whatever is put in front of me.

Another baby pigeon fell on the doorstep today. Precisely two years and two days after the last pigeon. It has been named Major. It is living in a shoe box.

I am not eating, sleeping nor walking. I struggled to stand long enough to pin my hair into place. I could not keep the concentration to read nor to complete any of my errands today. I shrugged around today, picking at the loose threads of the carpet and picking petty arguments. Tomorrow I shall try to appreciate London more, rather than being the ungrateful lump of dust that I am. I was tempted to do cocaine so I could read in peace as I cannot relax into anything. I might shut down tomorrow or one day soon, I can feel the creep.

Vomit in the aisle

The anxiety of spending two months in Brazil had gotten to me. But I hopped out of it (luckily) a week or so before. I prepared well but little. Three outfits, two gym sets, trainers, then my new brown leather shoes. I considered starting the diaries on the plane. I considered this before I even arrived at the airport, whilst I was still imagining my doings for the next few days.

I purposely did not imagine most things it seems — washing my face in a different mirror, meeting new people and speaking poor Portuguese, all of the things that bring the fear of God into me. I did not need to imagine anything, I puked my guts up in the aisle of the aeroplane, not for a fear of flying, but for something else unbalanced inside me. I had not imagined these scenarios — they slapped my cheeks and rendered me sweating on the plane floor.

But I am here now, for as long as I like. Last night I went to a Bahia restaurant, drank lemon and mint caipirinhas and ate prawn moqueqa. My stomach has recovered mostly after the stress of getting here. This morning I couldn't quite manage coffee or eggs, for I still feel a little on edge. I read a history of the world (HG Wells) at the bar of a bakery whilst I ate tapioca crepes with half a papaya. The cashier was wearing a black silk bow tie!

I had forgotten about the cables everywhere, disused electricity cables hang down, hundreds on each street, a black mess of wire from every post. It contributes to the business of São Paulo (SP). I do not like the tower blocks, but I love the trees on every street, not an oak in sight. Cactuses too. Saint George's Sword also very prominent.

I am sat in the kitchen drinking mate with peach (hot) as it is winter here—12 degrees in the morning, highs of 25 during the afternoon. I am nervous with things to do, my classes, my long-forgotten university work that I have not the slightest care for now. I haven't heard from them in months, for it's not their problem if I do not show up. I got good grades at the beginning of the year, I'll try and redo what I can later in the year when I have better routines. I got 85% in my last module—my poetry. But still I cannot care enough to go back and finish the degree.

I am doing better, I am exercising and reading most mornings. Today I do want to crawl back into bed, like I did as a young woman for the majority of the day. Two hours before lunch, I have the time, but I fear it is unwellness that makes me sleep. I wish I could read on the balcony in the sunshine, but it is cloudy today.

I am still living with a lot of fear inside of me. I doubt I will go to a cafe alone whilst in SP. I am enjoying the history of the world, it is talking about reptiles becoming birds with poor wings, reptiles suddenly showing an interest in their eggs rather than abandoning them to fend for themselves. I will read the bible for twenty minutes now, then have a small nap to set me up for the day. My stomach feels nervous writing about my life, although I am content right now.

Home days

All of life faded rather fast and I have despised myself here, especially amongst everyone else. In almost all company, I count to five to bring myself to look people in the eye, the people that are talking to me. Because of the language barrier, I can't help feel everyone talks at me, but I know this is my own problem.

A man sleeps outside the house most afternoons, he has a trailer you'd imagine a donkey would pull. I can't see anything in it other than cardboard. Even when I pass him, I despise myself. I despise those with more, and those with far less. I was invited to Bahia yesterday, but I only have money for food put aside. I cried in a bar with my head in my hands, for the reason that I did not ever work hard enough. I have barely worked two months in the last year. I make excuses I am not well, but then here in Brazil I have seen that in action. I am so overcome with my desperation for anything, I resort to a life of sleep, sometimes 20 hours a day. The last two days however have improved, I have stopped thinking so much about people going to Bahia and people sleeping on the street, I focus on moving.

Now the writing is making me miserable, I have no desire to express anything.

As coisas que me cercam

Me desinteresso pelas
paredes
janelas
pela rua
pelas pessoas.

Elas pesam demais
para mim.

Por isso mesmo
eu guardo lembranças vagas
livres do peso
livres da ternura

Distantes para lavar a alma.

Balcony

My bedroom is small but opens onto a balcony, with many plants. I swept the floor for the first time as I managed to crawl out of the bed before midday. Saint George's Sword and Jasmine, the other plants I couldn't tell you. Not that it matters too much. I wanted to buy more, but my money has dwindled fast.

The evening

Tapioca with guava and coconut
Peach mate w vodka
Agua de coco with ice
I care to the balcony
Spray the plants
Snip snip
Propagate the Jasmine
Clean linen

Then with godsent guilt
Caipirinhas in the pool
Wet linen
Wet kisses
Drive me into town
Seafood
Saint George's Sword everywhere
Reading in different rooms
Knowing I have someone
Of the same God.

Harmony

The first productive day in a long day, a real day, many people around me, good food, no booze. I wrote for eight hours, everything around me brought a smile or laughter, Brazil is treating me a little too well, don't you think?

Validation of writing? Writing for what? I cannot say, for I do not want to be restricted or restrained. But I continue to document my days each morning, sat beside the balcony, in the kitchen, with a pot of tea. Almost two months living in SP now. Every morning, a lot of fruit. A lot of agua de coco. Life is fine.

She is what some would describe a fussy girl. Although many would take to bed, for I can talk to most people with laughter and intimacy, if the mood takes me. She loves to be left to her own devices all day, to read on the doorstep in the stairs, eating tapioca and guava. She may be a difficult woman, but with many friends, many joys and a lot of pleasure. Listening to Jorge Ben Jor on headphones all afternoon. Painting a little. Following my baby around the world, doing his art. My little Penny girl. Brazil or God is kinder?

<u>Dinner party</u>

Morning exercise.
Laundry in the hot sun.
Lemon posset boiling on the stove.
Iced tea.
Family and friends over for dinner.
New (to me) green tweed dress.
Jasmine in a vase.
Tabouleh salad with sweet potato gnocchi,
Nutmeg in the flour.
If ruled by desire, we must die.
To be creations free of decay.
Minister our weary self and live as kindly to oneself as possible.

São Paulo, Brazil, 2023.

Drive out of town

"I prefer the vibe in the north-east" he said as we drove south, down through the grey cement metropolis. But in the middle of the highway there are flowers of red and pink, robust bushes nonetheless. A stinky river for the first few miles. Too stinky for Capybara, so my baby says. Then mountainous landscapes of green but fewer palms. To the left of the highway, a yellow faced favela. Further mountainous areas until you find smaller, condo style communities, deep with trees. My baby said he disagrees with the rich closed-off towns, naturally. The lukewarm bourgeois hate the hot bourgeois.

I have a litre of agua de coco for the journey and will soon stop at the Português restaurant for cod fish. The one at junction 53. The redhead boy that works there approached my table and said "how is my English red head sister?" And I told him I was happy to see my Brazilian red head brother. Incredibly handsome boy for his age, young 20s. We spoke three weeks ago, when I last came to the restaurant.

Car journeys still make my stomach weak. Smoked a lot before I left the house and took a Frontal ten minutes into the journey. Four hours remaining of the drive to Ourinhos (Little Gold).

In my bags I have Steppenwolf and The Well of Loneliness for the days by the pool.

Rant

I slept most of the day for feelings of foreign threat clouding my mind. I despise the wealthy, those living tucked away in houses filled to the top with tatt, absolute junk. Swimming pools surrounded by weeds. Children in the house until after 10pm, visiting and playing, at this time! They have the option to do morning or afternoon school, or both. Naturally they just do afternoons. There are maids to clean after every meal. Each area of the house is used and then left for the maid. I despise it all. Especially those that have maids. The loud music constantly. Television always on. The rotten photographs. The conversation extends to good day and good night. I enquired after a photo of a pilot on the wall, asking who it was, the answer I received was "a pilot". I have resorted to ignorance, pretending I do not speak or understand less than I do.

The food is very average outside of the city, but enough. Today we drove to a lake nearby to swim. I had to sit in the car for an hour, my bikini dripping cold water down my ass. The dogs bark constantly, ugly bull faced dogs with bulging eyes and bows in the hair. At least there are three cats here. I tried to make love to distract myself from my surroundings, but I am going to sleep early instead. I have no patience today. I fear I have no patience because it reminds me of Southery, a life of ignorance and those who demand so very little of their lives, content with their tv and maids to fill their days. I apologise for the nastiness. I purposely went back to bed and pretended to be asleep to avoid lunch with anyone today. But I did manage to read for an hour by the pool undisturbed. But if you had this much money, why build a house with a pool that only gets the sun until 11am? The water is too cool, despite it being a 32-degree day. I shall not grumble anymore. Although I'd rather be alone.

Fazenda

Leave evidence of your internal process in the world. I write to you.

Boisterously hot in Ourinhos today. Bright orange soil, the remains of an unknown volcano far before our time, according to him. It makes for fertile land, so surely is best for root vegetables? Instead, I see sugar cane, coffee, passion fruit and banana. Smashing mosquitoes and avoiding people still. Spent half an hour in the sun —before vacating indoors. My skin is terrible, agitated, and spotty, the entire time in Brazil. Nonetheless, I got ready around 14:00 to visit a friend's farm. I'm hoping they can laugh, have weed, and plenty of cold drinks on demand. Everyone else here has been stand-offish with me, probably a reflection of my bad moods these days. Wanting to return to SP, read in the studio, have drinks with friends and celebrate my birthday.

The fazenda was actually a highlight. The company was very light-hearted. They showed us around where their grandfather roasted coffee beans, banana trees, an old chapel, the cows. There was no electricity on the farm today, due to high winds. We smoked weed in the dark and the boys drank Cachaça.

Cotidiano

During the long car journeys, I daydream of jobless life in London, long afternoons in the flat, the lack of fruit. I would stay in Brazil for the food alone. If I was single, I would be so busy here. London feels not so much this way anymore, I've had enough time there.

Impatient of sitting in the flat, waiting for lunch time, time to go to the studio. I'd like to paint, read and smoke, all afternoon. It is not particularly warm, and I don't want to lounge, I want to vamos, but baby is working hard at home, and I must work on my patience. It wears thin. Cup of tea before lunch, write, edit, draw, walk. All of the world is outside of my door if I choose it today. I couldn't bring myself to exercise and did have a bong after breakfast, but I still want to keep busy.

Weeks is the swiftest of liminal waves, eight years into womanhood. The studios, the openings, the dinners, the sexual openness, swinging from trees, photographing your friends, renting a rowboat with all the people sat along the sides, like when we sat on the Seine. Then I am Elizabeth Bishop in my Brazil. I think of lovers as I lay in bed, then ask him for an orgy—for my birthday.

19th august (my birthday, age 26).

I am sat in a narrow tunnel of grey and brown. I imagine I am under a river, one of those mould holes you sit in very slowly. I haven't known hell so forcefully in the senses since this encounter. We are sat with the handbrake on, with a field of red every direction, everyone honking. It's tunnels, all I can think of. Tunnels I experienced as a child, mostly in the form of early airport drives to pick up grandma visiting from USA. Now in a tunnel to some collector's house, there's a party.

Baby looks like he's come from a ranch, but you cannot insult people here, for they are too sweet-hearted and headed. They enjoy any dialogue about themselves, in which they can promote their lifestyle, because people here have more hobbies and live better. I too have more than ever. Despite not keeping up with my Português, I am plenty busy. I shouldn't be so tired today, but I slept around 5am. Drank a lot of beer in the studio.

<u>Pinheiros balcony</u>

I bend down on the balcony
Bent low to lean and smoke a cigarette
My last evening on this balcony I cared for
For two months this care
My Jasmim and Saint George
Every day I tend to
I scrubbed on my knees this floor
My pristine garden
He closes the door
And complains of the smell
Says goodnight and disappears
As I return to London now.

My last day in Brasil

The world span too fast in front of me yesterday and rendered me sleepless. This morning upon making the bed, these sheets shrivelled and hurled into one corner, a bed of a useless night, you needn't inspect any further. I slept just two hours. I heard mosquitoes, that bothered me a lot. They hit my face every few minutes. I then rolled over every five minutes. My baby sent me home, he changed my ticket, and is sending me home tomorrow.

I didn't shower or wash my face, for I wanted to smell him on me, as I had done so the last few days or so. I was rendered sleepless but lustful.

So instead, I showered in the morning and washed my hair, put on my favourite socks, packed two pairs of shoes, a painting, some books, the signed Elizabeth Bishop from the man with the bookshop. The man that took me out a couple of times, or we'd mostly sit drinking outside of the bookshop, as it is on a parallel street to the house, a 30 second walk. I can see the roof from the balcony. We'd drink beer or wine on chairs outside the shop, until after 8pm, then he would walk me home, a sight that pained others more than I had originally thought—or not thought about at all.

Now retreat from behind my wall and be restless in other beds, my own, but I feel not for long. I shall have to move to shake my anxiety. Somewhere else in Hackney. I will try sobriety once home too. I will write often as I am writing you now, with candidness, for my respect for you, my melting wet love for you. So, he accidentally bought me a first-class ticket home when he changed my ticket so rapidly. I told him this morning and he was pissed off about it, I think it's all that was left.

But Monday has passed and today Tuesday I have no bed, just aeroplane until London mornings. I will visit the cat, unpack my bags, take a long bath, then I will go to the graveyard to paint watercolours and read. I will either stay the night in London for one night, or I will just head straight to Cambridge, to meet my mother. The usual movements I have come to know. I am lost in distance.

I hate travelling more than anything for my stomach and nerves are too delicate, I sweat and vomit on planes. He is pacing the room and not looking me in the eye.

E fiquei como quem não vive no mundo.
I was left as someone who doesn't live in this world.

Arrival in London

The night had eclipsed, and I can now see the squares of farmland from above. I slept the majority of the flight and did not eat, par one glass of champagne and a glass of chardonnay, just before sleeping. The difficulty of the flight, even in my window seat here, I am displaced. I return to London with again, nothing, nothing to do but write and try to make money, find a home to call my own, not lose it. I don't know if I'll make it to the country today, I would like to be alone and recover slowly alone here in London. I weeped during the flight on two occasions for no specific reason. My lack of affection for him, my lack of patience, my unpredictable taste, my unideal circumstances. But after all of this, I don't think I can feel the same in his vague, quiet world. My home of two years now, but he sent me away, banished me from his country, to effectively keep me away from men with bookshops.

I read his Elizabeth Bishop on the plane. I reanalysed holiday affairs and London affairs of my past. I need to be a single woman and that's it. Write letters from afar. I can be satisfied with that. I need a quiet life to myself for now.

I will arrive home very early in the morning, my rapid displacement. I intend to spend the day in and out of the bath. Brazil didn't have a bathtub.

Prince Albert

I write to you from Ely, at the table beside the bar, of my mother's pub. He told me not to spill my cider, but I told him I have been sitting here doing the same thing for seven years, master of nothing.

I over listen to conversations as I did when I was younger. I lived upstairs above the pub when I was 19 or so, alone in a large Victorian apartment. In the evenings when I was too depressed, I'd sit at this table and write as I do now.

We exchange messages constantly throughout the day. I try to keep entertained, I walked around the city, took photographs, spoke with him, sew and read Kafka and Cocteau diaries. He says I'm lucky to be in the country in my mother's pub. I say I feel I was extradited from Brazil, hence my hurt.

Xanax dreams

I awoke to the shouting of my name. I checked the time- just after 17:00. I immediately jolted up, and ran into the bathroom next door. My thighs and pyjamas were covered in menstruation, I quickly threw the pyjamas into the bin and sat on the floor of the shower.

I sat, recalling my dreams from my intense day of napping. I had been called to say goodbye to my baby, as he lay unable to move or speak, on the ground, in the back room of the studio. I made a fire on the ground, with stones to form a circle. My fire perked him up, we drank wine and he fell asleep. I then dreamt of islands, I was in Gibraltar. I was painting the air moving—there was a sandstorm. I painted only in a dark blue, the air and the sand. I had booked a restaurant for the evening and knew the owner (the man that has the coffee shop in the graveyard in Hackney)—I ordered oysters for my parents and orange wine. I confessed my love for him behind the bar, he said he felt the same and would see me in the evening. Shortly after, I was working in a hospital in Cambridge for humans with fleas. They said they could pay me £120 a week for working 4 nights, but I said that was fine, as I needed a job. Then the final dream, I was Queen Elizabeth's sister, sat beside her in a car. No idea where.

I returned to my 2x2 metre bedroom strewn with clothes, it was a warm day here and the room stank of menstruation. I pulled the duvet back over accordingly, and pushed my suitcase closed. Couldn't find any underwear, and I had only packed the one pair of trousers. Thank God for black! I had forgotten about periods and bodily functions the last few days. I looked

down to see the oil paint on my jeans. The pink of a
young girl love. The pink I used to paint with in Brasil
all afternoon, in the studio.

I tried to organise the various corners of my room. I'd
left a pile of writing paper, cards, receipts, and
medication on the bedside table. I quickly realised I did
not have much else to organise. I walked downstairs, as
I have not eaten or drank for 24 hours. I opened a can
of coke, my father-in-law shouted from the office "let
me see your face" so I said hello as swiftly as I could,
hiding my face with the can.

I thought of writing in the garden but returned to the
room. I thought of too going to the apple orchard as I
had promised myself, but I needed another day. I
thought I could sit against the tree to write, eat, drink,
and smoke until night-time, another three hours of
daylight or so. I even have cocaine in my pocket,
somebody gave me in the pub a few nights ago, but I'm
not so interested. I have a little money (I got a tax
rebate in the post!) so I could drink at the pub if I
wanted. Instead, I lay on the floor and listened to Jorge
Ben Jor, I slapped myself in the face as hard as I could
bare, then screamed into the carpet as loudly as I could
get away. I checked my phone to remember the last
time I had spoken to someone, or what I had said. I had
told him about the apple orchard, but consequently just
slept all day.

O dia acaba na tarde
A tarde acaba na noite
A noite acaba na madrugada
Na madrugada eu me acabo chorando.

They told me the hardship of life was due to the need for constant occupation. She had divorced him because she wanted to marry a journalist. Nobody had divorced me yet, but nobody had answered my phone calls today either.

Ordinary days in your hometown

Semi-productive day, the first day leaving the house in a while. Brushed my teeth with an aeroplane toothbrush, mine has mysteriously disappeared from my bags I have been living out of the past two months. A large burgundy leather handbag and a carry on suitcase. Four books, laptop, diary, notebooks, watercolours, needle and thread. He got off the plane this morning, he called me once home and said the cat is fine. He's the kind of person to brush his teeth on the plane. The kind of people that brush their teeth on planes are the type that carry a toothbrush to work. On a bus going across the fens, the hill of Haddenham and Wilburton meeting, where you can see flat across all the way to Cambridge, just briefly, six seconds or so out the window. We are going to meet in Cambridge next week, I bought tickets to Kettle's Yard for his birthday, then I'll take him for oysters, as tradition. My mouth tastes of copper for I scrubbed very hard, I'm on my way to the dentist. I hope they don't tell me off. I purposely wrote on my notes NERVOUS. I wish my tooth gap was a little bit bigger, it opens and closes over the years. It's a gap large enough to burn my gum on hot cheese. That's how you measure tooth gap.

Village bus

I thought of how on Wednesday you can read my immense letter of all, but I know I cannot force myself to write, nor be it much use for now, this week. Instead I bought you a birthday card with a Fenland dragon on. Inscribed something or another of the same effect, fulfilling life, many homes, here nor there, anywhere is fine for now, love you dearly.

The bus came from a different direction today, it takes two minutes to buy a ticket off a rackety shaky old man. His screensaver is a Down's syndrome little girl. When I worked in Paeds Oncology we had a lot of children with Down's on the ward, too in the care home. He drove the bus yesterday. He said my perfume was different today. Going into the fens via Witcham, Wentworth, Ely train station and onto the market square. I'll walk across the Palace Green and onto my mum's pub, where I said I'll work the night. I couldn't eat today, so I nearly didn't. But I bought a punnet of strawberries, green juice and bagels with butter. I watched tv to calm my nerves, so I could work. The air is fertile here and damp. The air reminds me of living here at 16 with long winter buses into Cambridge. There's mostly straw here now, as it is the first day of autumn. Arrived at the next village now, that has a notice board and six shelves of books at their bus stop. Plus a post box and a playing field. Lovely quaint village here Witcham. Never been here for any other reason than passing buses. Two women collected, early 60's, both wearing silver shoes.

Content note

This book contains themes of mental illness and references to suicidal ideation.

If you are affected by any of the themes discussed, I encourage you to contact Samaritans when life is difficult.

Samaritans are here–day or night, 365 days a year. You can call them for free on 116 123, email them at jo@samaritans.org, or visit www.samaritans.org to find your nearest branch.

Other international helplines can be found at www.befrienders.org.

Thoughts of men and self

Taste yourself and know yourself again. I have spent two or three days in a daze, and now by 9pm I must say goodbye to it, submit to the shower and sleep. For tomorrow I must return to waking up with purpose, moving, stretching and eating well. Just writing, exercise, eating well, trying to work on anything. No alcohol, no drugs (joint only in the evening). I am expecting a lot from one night but I am with a dull ache I must shake off, there is a lot I can do in two months. Still undecided where to live, missing the kitty but enjoying own company until 7pm or so. No appetite besides bread and butter, drinking beer, probably ovulating. Haven't made plans to meet anyone, staying quiet, reading in the garden and sleeping. Recollecting moments of sobriety in Brazil and the moments that led to it. Four vodkas deep in a motel. Humid days drinking of the street. Dancing in the studio. My favourite pastime. Dancing alone that is. Can still only listen to the same few songs or so on repeat. The same songs I'd listen to on the balcony in Brazil, when I had my goodnight farewell cigarette to the night and return to sleep next to him. Must return back to self—experimentally I am empty and transparent, even when I forget, still and at peace, if I chose to mould such a woman.